2 Corinthians

you are the rig...

of God in Christ

Love!
Sis Sharon

# Bringing
# HOPE

### Life-Changing
### Wisdom *for* Christ Followers

## LIZ MORRIS
*and*
### The Dallas Dream Team

*Cover Design and Interior Layout and Design | JOSEP Designs*
*Cover Photography: Sergy Nivens (c) 123RF.com*

**BRINGING HOPE**
**LIFE-CHANGING WISDOM FOR CHRIST-FOLLOWERS**
Liz Morris and *The Dallas Dream Team*

Copyright 2020
Published by Your Voice Matters
A Division of *The Dallas Dream Team*
Plano, Texas
www.thedallasdreamteam.com

ISBN (Print):    978-1-7344545-0-5
ISBN (Ebook):    978-1-7344545-1-2

# CONTENTS

# DEDICATION

T he *Dallas Dream Team* would like to dedicate our very first devotional to *Cornerstone Crossroad Academy,* the first non-profit recipient of our grant, and to *Salvation Today,* the first missionary award recipient.

The work they do is incredibly inspiring, uplifting and rewarding. They will forever be in our hearts as we continue to serve the 'least of these', both in our community and all over the world. Thank you for your hard work and commitment to the Lord, Jesus Christ. May He richly recompense you with many eternal rewards and crowns.

# SPECIAL THANKS

We recognize and thank *Mary Ethel Eckard*, one of *The Dallas Dream Team's* most gifted and dedicated members, for the outstanding job of compiling and editing this devotional. Mary willingly and wholeheartedly donated her time and talents to complete this project. Pursuing over one hundred women to submit a devotional on time is a difficult challenge, but she never gave up - even though she had to extend the deadline three times. Mary spent countless hours reading, editing, designing and arranging the flow of this endeavor without complaint. She recruited the help of *Gloria Ashby* to help with final edits, and we are thankful for their partnership that produced our first

*Dallas Dream Team* publication. Words will never express our gratitude, Mary, for the work you have done in compiling these stories so lives can be transformed. Thank you from all of us, and thanks for making us all sound like professional writers. Job well done!

# FOREWORD

Liz Morris and I have been close friends for over 22 years, attending church together, celebrating occasional holidays as families, and watching each other's children grow. It's funny because, in many ways, we are very different in giftings and personality. I'm artistic, but I am also an analytical, deep thinker who can stay home with books and teaching plans and be perfectly happy. Liz is a dynamic, no-holds barred, world-conquering racehorse with a mind for business, and a plethora of friends - all of whom adore her.

We're quite different, and yet Liz and I have been best friends for a long time. Why? Many reasons, but the main one is our love for Jesus Christ and all that pertains to His kingdom. We've spent many hours on the phone, in restaurants, and on small trips together, chasing God and contemplating His kingdom. She would get a word, then I would get a word, and together we would squeal like school girls, getting goose bumps over the revelations God had given.

And we both share a passion for the supernatural. The Bible says signs and wonders are to follow every believer, so this is something we have longed for and sought after. In fact, this is the singular, extraordinary thing that separates God's kingdom from the rest of the world. He's called us to bring Heaven to earth, just as His Son did.

As an enthusiast, Liz has many ideas. But in 2018, she approached me with a very special one, a concept for a ministry she would call *The Dallas Dream Team*. This particular idea was genius in its simplicity – the assembling of faithful donors as members, then choosing an existing

Christian nonprofit to be awarded a substantial grant each year. This was a no-brainer to me, so uncomplicated, yet so effective in boosting the finances of the winning charity - one whose work is greatly affecting those in need in the Dallas area. I quickly jumped on board and have been serving ever since.

The beauty of *The Dallas Dream Team* is the blend of beautiful Christian ladies it has bound together ... people with a heart to please God and have an effect in their community. I've been privileged to become acquainted with so many dear sisters I would have never known had it not been for *The Dallas Dream Team*! I think it's wonderful that these women, so united in Spirit, get to share stories and insights through this book. I thank both God and Liz for providing this opportunity, and I pray the reader is blessed and inspired by the heartfelt reflections printed in each devotion. May God perform miracles in the pages of this book!

Sheila Ninowski
Vice President / Treasurer
*The Dallas Dream Team*

# INTRODUCTION

*But seek ye first his kingdom, and his righteousness; and
all these things shall be added unto you. Matthew 6:33*

## A Rescue Mission

In the summer of 2017, I received a phone call from the President of
a non-profit street ministry inviting me to participate in a rescue
mission. I was to wear closed-toe shoes to reduce the risk of being
stuck by hypodermic needles. We were headed into one of the most
dangerous areas of Dallas, where a murder had been committed a few
days before.

Because the rescue mission was risky, we required police surveillance.
We encountered people whose lives were compromised, including
pimps, prostitutes, sex trafficked teenagers, transvestites, gang bangers,
drug users, call girls, sex slaves and watchers. Though we were there to
share the love of Christ, our words were limited, so we demonstrated His
love through our actions. By God's divine presence and intervention,
our ministry team rescued five people.

The experience changed me. My heart was burdened for those whose
lives were upside down from what God wanted, and a passion stirred
within me to make a positive impact. But how could I be part of a
movement to change the Dallas community with the love of Christ? I

visited several mission sites including The Salvation Army and Union Gospel Mission. I visited with women who had been sexually exploited, and I listened as they shared their stories. God presented two things to me: a great need and a great opportunity. Through prayer and the study of other funding organizations, I realized the impact could be made one charity at a time. The answer? The formation of *The Dallas Dream Team*.

## The Dallas Dream Team

Founded in 2018, *The Dallas Dream Team*'s mission is to make a difference, an imprint for all eternity, in the lives of people who need a rescue, but whom most of us will never encounter. We are a sisterhood comprised of women from all walks of life, along with corporate sponsors. We contribute grants to aid non-profits in the Dallas area who spread the gospel of Jesus Christ while ministering to those who need a fresh start.

At the time of this publication, *The Dallas Dream Team* has over 150 members. Our goal is to increase the team to one million members so we can reach one million souls. One hundred percent of funds go directly to the non-profit ministries. For more information about *The Dallas Dream Team*, visit our website at www.thedallasdreamteam.com.[1]

## Bringing Hope

When the idea of a devotional was introduced as a fundraiser, my first thought was, 'this book needs to be life-changing. I want the women involved to share something that will make a difference in the lives of others.'

We gathered stories, lessons and experiences from the members of *The Dallas Dream Team*. These devotions range from defeat to victory, from struggles to faith, from selfishness to godliness. The stories and lessons are shared from the hearts of those who long to be more like Christ, to glorify Him in their decisions, and to surrender to Him their sinful desires in exchange for His purpose and plan. Throughout the book, you will glean wisdom and understanding about some of the Keys to the Kingdom. What are these keys?

## Five Keys to the Kingdom

Key to the Kingdom #1: God wants your participation. How do you participate? Working through this devotional is a good step. Each day grab your Bible and look up the referenced scriptures in each story. Work through the action items at the end of each reading. Journal your thoughts or questions. Pray and ask God to give you wisdom about the scripture and the devotionals. Does the scripture or story provide guidance you need for a situation in your life? How can you apply what you have read?

Key to the Kingdom #2: Understand that we are all on a journey with the Holy Spirit. You will see the depths of some of the stories and the beauty in the beginnings of other stories. God does not put pressure on the pace of your growth, but He does desire it. Each person is at a different place in their walk with the Father, so read the stories with a desire to learn from others.

Key to the Kingdom #3: Spend time in God's presence. Without hearing His voice and direction, you can make decisions and seek counsel from people who know nothing about God's divine plan for you. How can you follow anything that is not inspired by the Father? Jesus never did. How do you do this? Talk to Him. Take Him everywhere you go. Ask Him questions and wait for His reply. He will answer and it will sound like your voice. He sometimes interrupts your thoughts. His voice is identifiable and the more you talk to Him, the more you learn to recognize His voice and hear His answer. The Bible tells us in John 10:27, "My sheep hear my voice and I know them, and they follow me."

Key to the Kingdom #4: Understand the spiritual authority of being God's child. God's Kingdom has no end. He is a King who loves to please

His people. He desires that we walk in His authority, casting down evil entities that try to take over His loved ones.

Key to the Kingdom #5: Develop and maintain deep and purposeful spiritual connections with other Christ-followers. God created us to be in relationship with others, just as we are with Him. Surround yourself with people at different levels of spiritual maturity; some to mentor, some to be your mentor, and some to accompany you through life's journey.

## Nuggets of Truth

As you begin this devotional journey, listen, discern, pray and read scripture. Work through the action items. In your quiet place, ask the Holy Spirit for wisdom. This is the only way to learn and apply God's Keys to His Kingdom. Throughout this devotional you will receive simple nuggets that further explain these and other Keys to the Kingdom, and how to use them for your spiritual growth and maturity. Pay attention. They will be life-changing.

If you have a story to share, or would like additional information about *The Dallas Dream Team,* let us know by filling out the "Get in Touch" form at https://thedallasdreamteam.com/contact/. Be assured, *Your Voice Matters.*

Liz Morris, President and Founder
*The Dallas Dream Team*

*"One million dollars for one million souls."*

# FROM BULLIED TO BELOVED

*You are the God who sees me. Genesis 16:13*

In middle school, I was bright, shy and introverted, and felt like a square peg. I was unattractive with a lazy eye that stayed to the side and a jaw abnormality that kept my mouth from closing properly, giving the appearance of having buck teeth. Students teased and bullied me, calling me names like "dog face." My lazy eye was corrected in sixth grade, but the bullying didn't stop.

I was embarrassed by the way I looked. I had no self-esteem, no self-confidence and, eventually, became angry and vengeful. I began having thoughts about hurting the people who bullied me, and I felt justified in those thoughts, though I never acted on them.

In high school, our family relocated to another city. I had hopes that, at a new school, people would see me instead of judging me. My hopes vanished the first day of school, when two boys pointed and laughed, teasing me about my appearance. I was humiliated, my heart was heavy, and I felt empty. I decided to turn off my emotions and never allow anything to hurt me again.

My personality changed that day. I began using drugs and lost all motivation. Though I worked part-time, made good grades and had a few friends, I was emotionally disengaged. I was paralyzed with fear that no matter what I did, I would give people more ammunition to tease me and put me down. I existed but had no life in me.

Before my senior year of high school, I had surgery to fix the jaw issue, which made a big difference in my appearance. When I returned to school, I was unrecognizable. People told me I was pretty. I didn't know how to receive their compliments and felt unworthy of them. My outside appearance had changed, but my inside was still dark, wounded, and hurting. I had no self-confidence or self-esteem and continued to behave in ways that caused people to reject me.

Eventually I met my husband. I couldn't figure out what he saw in me, as I thought I was awkward, nerdy and unattractive. But he didn't see me that way. He was the first person to make me feel accepted for who I was. Early in our marriage, we gave our hearts to Christ, and I began to find peace. Something changed on the inside, but I still behaved in ways that brought rejection and judgment.

We started attending church and learning about God. I enrolled in a class called *The Search for Significance*. We studied fear of rejection, failure, shame, and other mindsets that hold us back. I learned that all the years of teasing made me ashamed of who I was and made me hate myself, inside and out. I shared my story with the class, and to my surprise, they understood my hurt. Two days later, I started crying, and I grieved the pain for over an hour. I knew God was pulling out all the junk buried deep inside. Afterwards, I felt light and free, like a different person. I didn't recognize myself. I was full of joy for the first time in my life. God removed my pain and healed the emotional wounds I carried for years. Over time, my personality was transformed. My self-esteem and self-confidence were restored. Our God is a God of restoration. He brings beauty from ashes if we allow Him to work in our lives.

Contributing Writer | Elizabeth Broz

## *Action, Application, Accountability*

Scripture teaches we are to pursue love. Today, choose to show love to someone you would otherwise avoid or tease. Your life will increase as you practice this principle of pursuing love, not worrying about the outcome or the judgment of others. Journal about your experience.

# Uniquely Designed

*For we are God's workmanship, created in Christ
Jesus to do good works, which God prepared
in advance for us to do. Ephesians 2:10*

Have you ever pondered what it means to be God's workmanship? He is proud of you, His creation, His masterpiece. God lovingly knit you together in your mother's womb (Psalm 139). No part of you is a mistake. Have you stopped to sense His love for you today? He took great care to design each part of you, each preference, each strength, and each unique attribute. Do you believe God uniquely designed you?

You were created on purpose for a purpose. The world is filled with numerous conferences, assessments, books and sermons about finding your purpose. Each of these resources can enlighten you about your design, but that is not enough. In order to walk in the good works God has for you, you must spend time communing with God and listening to His Holy Spirit.

The Spirit will lead you into the good works that were planned specifically for you. If you have ever longed for significance in your life, take heart! God *wants* to use you. He will lead you each day as you make time for Him. Live with expectation that God will use you as you listen to Him and obey. He longs to work through you. Good works flow out of our intimacy with God. Using our God-given gifts to glorify Him is a joy!

But, be careful. Don't be confused and only value your life based on a list of roles, goals and spiritual to-do lists. Your focus can get off track when you are overly concerned with "doing." God cares more about being with you. It is in this intimate communion that you enjoy His presence and hear what is on His heart. You were designed to know Him intimately. Remember our Father was "well pleased" with Jesus before Jesus began his ministry.

*As soon as Jesus was baptized, he went up out of the water. At that moment heaven was opened, and he saw the Spirit of God descending like a dove and lighting on him. And a voice from heaven said, "This is my Son, whom I love; with him I am well pleased." Matthew 3:16-17*

He loves to spend time with you, to fellowship with you. Don't let your prayer time become a long list of requests you want God to accomplish. Will you choose to take a moment today to hear what God wants to talk to you about? May you experience God's deep abiding love today before you "do" anything.

Contributing Writer | Alisa Evans
Executive Director, Alive at Last

## *Action, Application, Accountability*

Take a moment and ask Jesus what He loves about your unique design. Ask Him how you can partner with Him today. It is up to you to stop, breathe and listen for His still small voice.

# EXCHANGE POLICY

*What can a man give in exchange for his soul? Mark 8:37*

When I was a young girl, I couldn't wait to receive the newest issue of the Sears Roebuck Catalog. I spent countless hours poring over the images of ladies dressed in beautiful clothes. I thumbed through pages and pages of toys, beautiful home décor, and camping equipment.

My father purchased much of the camping equipment for our family outings from the pages of those colorful catalogs. He was impressed with the quality of their merchandise and the fact they stood behind their products. Sears and Roebuck's liberal return and replacement policy allowed returns on anything purchased from them, no matter its current condition or purchase date. No questions asked.

We knew a family who purchased a tent, used it for several years and, when they no longer planned on camping, boxed it in its original carton and returned it to the store. They received a full refund of their original purchase price. If you purchased Sears' Craftsman tools and they wore out, Sears would replace them with a new tool, free of charge.

God is a lot better than Sears and Roebuck. He freely gave Adam and Eve the gift of a brand-new perfect life in the Garden of Eden. He allowed them the use of that life to do as they chose, with only one warranty instruction, "Do not eat from one particular tree in the garden."

When they violated the terms of this warranty, they were forced to return their perfect life and receive a replacement, far inferior to the original. But there was one important clause to this return policy. At the moment of this exchange of a perfect life for a defective one, God promised Adam and Eve there would come a time when they would be able to reclaim their perfect life and be restored to perfection. (Genesis 3:15)

When God told Satan that Eve's Seed would bruise his head, He promised that from her lineage a Savior would come who would restore His children to a brand-new perfect life forever. When He sent Jesus to die on the cross, He kept that promise.

You don't have to go to some hard-to-reach location and stand in line to complete this exchange transaction. You can do it right here, right now, right where you are. All you need to do is surrender your worn out, broken, used and defective life to Him, and receive a guarantee, right on the spot. What is that guarantee? One day you will walk restored to perfection with Him in heaven, for eternity.

Contributing Writer | Sue Arrington

## *Action, Application, Accountability*

If you are looking for the guarantee mentioned above, you can begin your walk with Christ right here, right now, right where you are. How? By believing in Jesus and inviting Him to be part of your life. You can pray, "Dear Jesus, I know that I am a sinner and I ask for Your forgiveness. I believe You died for my sins and rose from the dead. I turn from my sins and invite You to come into my heart and life. I want to trust and follow You as my Lord and Savior. Amen."

# HATRED TO LOVE

*What Israel sought so earnestly it did not obtain, but the elect did. The others were hardened, as it is written: "God gave them a spirit of stupor, eyes so that they could not see and ears so that they could not hear, to this very day." Romans 11:7–8*

I was born and raised in the Middle East in a devout Muslim family. From a young age, I was taught to despise the Jewish people and refer to them as "Yahoudi", a disrespectful term in Arabic. Though I never met or experienced harm from a Jewish person, when I heard the word "Yahoudi," my young heart filled with hatred and resentment toward them. Muslim history teaches that Jews are to be rejected and the nation of Israel is the land of Palestinian people. I didn't realize the God of Israel had given the whole land of Israel to the Jewish people forever. Never once did I think to question my family or Islam's teachings.

Eight years after coming to the United States, someone gave me a Bible. Two years after I began reading it, the blinders fell away and the truth was revealed. In Genesis 12:2-3, the Lord said to Abram, "I will make you into a great nation and I will bless you; I will make your name great, and you will be a blessing, I will bless those who bless you, and whoever curses you I will curse; and all peoples on earth will be blessed through you." Then I read, "The people of Israel, theirs is the adoption as sons; theirs the divine glory, the covenants, the receiving of the law, the temple worship and the promises." (Romans 9:4)

I came to believe Yeshua was who He claimed to be, the One born in Israel, who gave His life on the cross in Israel, and who rose from the grave in Israel, the Savior of the World and the Messiah of Israel. I rejected Islam and became a follower of Yeshua. It was also revealed that Jesus has a Jewish heritage and He loves Israel and calls them His chosen people. It became clear that the God of the Bible saw the Jewish people differently than I had been taught. I read about how much He loved and blessed them, and how He performed miracles for them throughout history. In the book of Exodus, I learned how God delivered the children of Israel from their Egyptian captivity and miraculously provided them with food and water in the desert. In the Old Testament, He made a covenant with the Jewish people, over and over. The moment I realized the Jews were God's chosen people and His special possession, my heart began to break for them. I fell to my knees and asked the Lord to forgive my hatred toward His people. God began developing His love for the Jews in my repentant heart.

A few years ago, I was given an opportunity to travel to Israel to share my story with Holocaust Survivors. This was a pivotal point because the Holy Spirit gave me the desire to reach out to these who had suffered so greatly. I shared my story of how Yeshua came into my life and replaced my lifelong hatred with His great love. As the Holy Spirit spoke through me, I asked them to forgive my people (the Arabic Muslim people) for their hatred of the Jewish people. I explained that they were blinded to the truth because, unlike me, they have not been transformed by the love of Yeshua. After I spoke, many in the audience were weeping. They made their way to meet me, using canes and walkers. With tears in my eyes, I embraced them all. It was a day of celebration-reconciliation watching God restore and mend broken hearts as only He can. Since then, I have heard many testimonials of salvation among the Jewish Holocaust Survivors. Now I see through the eyes of compassion and mercy, not rejection and hatred. There is a spiritual battle for the souls of God's chosen people, and one day, His people will be set free.

Contributing Writer | Safeeya
Watch Safeeya's story at https://www.youtube.com/watch?v=wzfVAb4q8ZU

## *Action, Application, Accountability*

If there is hatred in your heart, it is because of lies the enemy has instilled in you. Jesus wants to take that away. Confess your sin, seek His forgiveness, and ask Him to give you His heart of love for all people.

# KEEP PEDALING

*Therefore, since we are surrounded by such a great cloud*
*of witnesses, let us throw off everything that hinders*
*and the sin that so easily entangles, and let us run with*
*perseverance the race marked out for us. Hebrews 12:1*

D ad strolled out of the garage with a wrench in his hand while I biked up and down the sidewalk. He stopped at the end of our driveway and waved the wrench toward my training wheels. "You're ready to take those off." I wasn't so sure. My six-year-old feet barely reached the pedals dad built up with wooden blocks on my new bike. As he unscrewed the bolts that attached the training wheels, Dad shot me a fatherly smile and said, "You got this. You can balance on your own now."

Training wheels tossed aside, we walked to the middle of the street. Mom stood at the opposite end, two house-lengths away. My sister, brother, and neighborhood friends lined the curb to watch me take flight or crash onto the pavement. I straddled the bike, just tall enough to peer over the handlebars. "Ride straight toward Mom," Dad said. "I'll run beside you and hold the back of the seat until you get your balance. Ready?"

I took three deep breaths, put my right foot on the pedal, and pushed it forward. As the right pedal went down, my left foot caught the rising left block of wood. I pumped in a circular motion but wobbled, struggling to point the front wheel toward Mom. As promised, Dad ran beside me, holding my seat to keep me balanced.

Halfway to Mom, he let go. I panicked. I forgot to pedal, and the front wheel swerved wildly back and forth. "Keep pedaling. Keep going. You're doing fine." Dad's words came from behind me. I held the handlebars steady and pedaled with all my might. The front wheel stopped wobbling. I reached Mom and rode past her, grinning from ear to ear.

That memory comes to mind whenever I embark on something new, like staring into the face of a daunting challenge or riding into a new season of life. Like when I no longer relied on parents for financial help, or switched career paths to answer my heart's passion, or retired. That's when I remember my father assuring me, "You're ready." With each change – whether by choice, calling, or circumstance – I reach a crossroads in faith. Then, I hear my Father-God say, "You've practiced enough. Let's take those training wheels off." I discover He has equipped me with whatever He calls me to do. Though I may wobble at first, His Holy Spirit reminds me, "You got this. Just keep pedaling."

Contributing Writer | Gloria Ashby

## *Action, Application, Accountability*

Jesus wants you to grow in faith so miracles can be released. If you stay in your comfort zone, you will never obtain the greatness of the future God has for you. When you get involved with Him, He becomes involved with you. Remove the training wheels of your life and trust Him. He runs alongside to hold you up. Grab some courage and step out in obedience to God's promptings. You will hear Him say, "You got this, just keep trusting."

# BALANCE

*Answer me when I call to you, O my righteous God.*
*Give me relief from my distress; be merciful to me and*
*hear my prayer. I will lie down and sleep in peace, for you*
*alone, O Lord, make me dwell in safety.* *Psalm 4:1, 8*

I grew up in a domestically abusive home with my parents and five siblings. My mother instilled God's Word in us and found comfort involving us in church services, knowing it was a safe environment. Though she tried to shield us as much as possible, living in an abusive situation brought challenges throughout life. My childhood and adult years were shadowed by lack of self-esteem and fear, which in many ways stunted my emotional growth. Hiding from the past seemed easier than facing it and allowing the pain to be faced and healed.

There is a point in life, if we live long enough, when events unfold that bring the wounds and pains from the past to the present. This happened to me in my 59th year. Within a twelve-month period, I suffered from heart failure, a stroke, and surgery to repair the heart damage. As I was healing from the physical ailments, I lost my home and all my belongings in a fire.

The loss of physical health and personal treasures found me at a crossroads of faith. Did I truly believe what scripture said about God's love and provision? The Bible teaches that with faith the size of a mustard seed, all things are possible. Having nowhere else to go, I leaned into

God and the promises I had been taught as a young child. As I grieved the loss of so many things, the pain and wounds from my childhood and early adult years surfaced. It seemed God had me in a time of healing that would close the door from the abusive past and set me on the path to wholeness. Hindsight revealed how God had to move me to save me. He had to orchestrate loss to gain me freedom from fear.

Contributing Writer | Yvonne Alford

## Action, Application, Accountability

Here are three powerful lessons I learned during this season, perhaps these can help you too.

1. Accept your life and circumstances. Allow God to heal you. He can use everything you have experienced to grow you into the person He created you to be and to help others.
2. Stand strong in His promises. Remember, He is with you. He hears you when you call, and He has a plan and a purpose for your life.
3. Advocate for yourself, knowing He stands with you along the way. He loves you and gives you wisdom and confidence to speak, live, and walk in His ways.

# ANGEL IN THE AIRPORT

*O Lord, you are my God; I will exalt you and praise
your name, for in perfect faithfulness you have done
marvelous things, things planned long ago. Isaiah 25:1*

Early in our marriage we lived in Wisconsin. My husband, Brad,
had a job opportunity that would move us to Texas. He was
excited, but I was apprehensive. He suggested I travel to Dallas
with our six-month-old daughter, Katrina, and, if I liked the area, we
would move.

Traveling with an infant includes lugging a car seat, suitcases, and
a diaper bag. There was no way I could carry everything by myself. I
reasoned, if God wanted me to go to Texas, He would have to intervene.
And I had peace about it. I assumed the Lord would get me a parking
spot next to the elevator, but there were none. I finally found a spot in
the desolate remote parking, far from the elevators. I knew I could not
walk blocks to the elevator and then leave the suitcases while I retrieved
Katrina in her car seat. Was this God's answer?

As I parked, I didn't see anyone in the parking lot who could help.
I stepped out of the van to survey the situation, and immediately heard
a voice behind me. I spun around to see a clean-cut slender man in a
dark blue suit. I was startled. Where did he come from? He asked, "Can
I help you carry your things?" Wide-eyed, I answered, "Yes, I would very
much appreciate help."

He took the suitcases and I carried Katrina in her car seat along with the monster diaper bag. We walked to the elevator. He was quiet and I was distracted with thoughts of how to navigate the airport. I now wish I had asked a few questions, like, where he came from or why he didn't have his own luggage. We walked to the check-in desk at the lower level. After putting the car seat down, I looked up to thank him, and he was gone. I scanned the hall, back and forth, and he was nowhere to be seen. He simply disappeared.

We made it to Dallas, fell in love with the state, and moved to Texas. It is here the Lord had a plan to grow our family and fulfill His purpose. It was a critical life changing move, we thank the Lord for His leading and provision, and for the angel in the airport.

Contributing Writer | Kathleen Watson

## Action, Application, Accountability

I challenge you, submit your hopes and dreams to the Lord. He is a loving faithful God who desires to be involved in the lives of His children. Then heed His voice and trust His leading. He will provide and equip you with whatever you need to get you wherever He wants you to go.

# Don't Look Back

*Forget the former things; do not dwell on the past. See,
I am doing a new thing! Now it springs up; do you
not perceive it? I am making a way in the wilderness
and streams in the wasteland. Isaiah 43:18-19*

Remember Lot's wife? She "looked back" and was turned into a pillar of salt. (Genesis 19:26) Jesus warned us not to be like Lot's wife by focusing on the past.

This is a hard one. I tend to wake up in the middle of the night, replaying scenes from my life that did not go well, turning them over and over in my mind. Mistakes I made, people I hurt or irritated, actions I could have handled differently, etc. I worry about the worst of them for *years*. I suspect I'm not alone.

- What causes us to look back?
- Why is it so hard to focus on the present?
- What can we do to avoid the tendency to look back?

Jesus told us that worrying will not accomplish anything, it is a useless endeavor. We need to remember who we are and whose we are. For those with faith, we *know* God takes our sins and mistakes and weaves them into a beautiful tapestry.

So, what can we do to dissipate memories of the past or worries that surface, like a thief in the night, to rob us of sleep? Once I recognize I have fallen into the trap of looking back and worrying, I repeat, "Jesus! Help me calm my tangled thoughts. Help me sleep." Sometimes I choose a favorite Bible verse and repeat it. This simple practice helps break the negative thought pattern, engage the Lord who is always near, and restore a focus on the present. I almost never fail to fall asleep.

Contributing Writer | Rebecca Campbell

## *Action, Application, Accountability*

When you find your thoughts turning to worry and fear, engage your mind with prayer and scripture. The power of conversation with God and the repetition of scripture replaces worry and fear with hope and encouragement.

# WORRY

*Who of you by worrying can add a single
hour to his life?* Matthew 6:27

Worry affects everyone. We worry about our kids, our husbands, our work, the house, the dog, and finances. It never ends. Sometimes we have larger things to worry about, like an ailing parent, the loss of a job, a child who is choosing the wrong path. Worry seems to be a part of our everyday life. By feeding it and allowing it to grow, it takes root in our minds.

I'll never forget a time when this was proven to me. When I was 22, I had a miscarriage. It was the most devastating time in my life. Shortly thereafter, I unexpectedly became pregnant again. I was petrified. I was so wrought with worry that I would miscarry again that I cried myself to sleep every night. It was terrible. It was all I could think about. The worry consumed me. Each night I would plead with the Lord for my baby to be healthy.

One night, I lay in bed, praying and crying yet again. Suddenly, I heard the Lord say, "You are fine and your baby is fine. Do not worry." I physically felt a huge weight lifted. From that point on, I wasn't anxious about anything during the pregnancy. It was such an odd feeling to go from being consumed with worry to absolute confidence. It was freeing and wonderful. Only the Lord could have made the 180-degree change in my heart and mind.

We waste so much time and energy on worry, when really, what does it accomplish? Absolutely nothing. How is worrying going to fix anything? It won't, it just feeds the negativity.

The good news is, God is in control. Rather than wasting time on worry, hand your troubles to the Lord and use it to build your faith. Worry won't change your situation, but God can and will, just like He did with me. God takes care of all His creatures, even the birds. "Look at the birds of the air; they do not sow or reap or store away in barns, and yet your heavenly Father feeds them. Are you not much more valuable than they?" (Matthew 6:26). If God takes such good care of the birds, rest assured He will take great care of you.

Contributing Writer | Stephanie Chavez

## *Action, Application, Accountability*

God's got you. Rather than being a worrier, be an encourager. You are medicine for someone's wound. You are a seed. Sow your caring. What you make happen for others, God will make happen for you. Words stop storms, halt worries, and change lives. Sow words of kindness in someone's life today. You never know the difference your positive words can make.

# ARE MIRACLES STILL
# HAPPENING TODAY?

*I tell you the truth, anyone who has faith in me will do what
I have been doing. He will do even greater things than
these, because I am going to the Father. John 14:12*

At twenty-five and newly married, my husband and I attended church in Little Rock, Arkansas. The Pastor was a man of great faith and believed in all the gifts of the Holy Spirit. One Wednesday evening after teaching, he asked anyone needing prayer to come to the front of the church. As Jeff and I sat on the second pew with our eyes closed, two women walked to the front of the church and sat on the pew directly in front of us.

The Holy Spirit spoke to me. "The woman in front of you is pregnant and her baby is deformed. If you lay your hands on her, by your faith I will heal the child." His voice was so clear, it was almost audible. I lifted my head to see if anyone was speaking to me and was surprised to see the two women on the pew ahead. Immediately the devil put a thought in my head, "How do you know she is pregnant?" Doesn't that sound familiar? Just like when he spoke to Eve in the garden when he asked her, "Did God really say...?"

I placed my hand on her shoulder, bowed my head, and prayed for her baby. As soon as I finished, the pastor motioned for the woman to come for prayer. As she stood, I could see she was about eight months pregnant. If I had been standing, my knees would have buckled. He handed the microphone to the woman and she said, "As you can see, I am pregnant. I had a sonogram today and was told my baby doesn't have legs." As soon as I heard her words, I knew God had spoken and I had responded in obedience. I was confident the baby would be born with legs.

After the service, I told Jeff what happened. His first reaction was, "Oh my goodness, we need to keep praying for her." But the Holy Spirit gave me peace it was already done, so I told Jeff there was no need for us to pray again.

The following Wednesday night at church, the Pastor asked for praise reports from the congregation. A woman came to the front of the church and said, "I was here last Wednesday night with my daughter, and you all prayed for her. She was the pregnant one and her baby's legs were deformed." Jeff nudged my leg, and we both waited in anticipation. She continued, "My daughter went back to the doctor today and had another sonogram. The baby's legs were there."

That day my life changed radically. Please hear me. Miracles are for today. We only need faith to believe. If we believe in Jesus this is our inheritance.

Contributing Writer | Liz Morris

## Action, Application, Accountability

Devote time each day in God's Word, reading it from cover to cover. True understanding comes when you invite the Holy Spirit to be your teacher and guide as you read scripture. He alone can give the understanding in a way that will touch your heart and teach you through your circumstances.

# WHO TOLD YOU, YOU WERE NAKED?

*I delight greatly in the Lord; my soul rejoices in my God.
For he has clothed me with garments of salvation and
arrayed me in a robe of righteousness. Isaiah 61:10*

I n the garden of Eden, Adam and Eve walked and talked with God in the cool of the day. While there, they were deceived by the serpent, and chose to eat from the Tree of the Knowledge of Good and Evil. With that, everything changed and their innocence was taken away. Their fateful decision caused death to enter. After that, the first emotion Adam and Eve experienced was shame. They felt ashamed of their nakedness and chose to cover what was once pure, innocent, and beautiful. When God came looking for them, they hid. This was also the first time they experienced fear. This should be a signal that when we operate in shame or fear, we experience emotions that originated from death. Let that sink in.

The real story is this: When God called out to them, Adam answered, trying to explain what happened, expressing his fear due to his sense of nakedness. Even in modern times, we may say we feel "naked" in certain situations. This expression usually portrays a sense of not being enough, not being prepared, or feeling vulnerable.

God replied to Adam with a rhetorical question, asking, "Who told you, you were naked?" Obviously, God wasn't asking this question for an answer. He was stressing a point. Like a parent who spends years raising his child, nurturing and encouraging him, God gently chided him with exasperation. His point was, "Who on earth told you to be ashamed? I would not tell you to be ashamed of your bodies, or anything else, for that matter. I would not condemn or make you feel insecure." God's question was an emphatic, "Why did you listen to someone else? Someone who doesn't love you, instead of Me, the One who truly does? Why did you believe in someone else's lies? Why wouldn't you trust Me, the One who created you, has encouraged you, empowered you, and believed in you all this time?"

Shame is not just an emotion from doing something wrong. Shame is deeper. Shame makes us feel unworthy, stupid, ugly, incapable, or undervalued. Shame diminishes us in our mind, and as such, is damaging to our well-being. Shame robs us of confidence, peace, joy, and the satisfaction of realizing the magnificent masterpiece God created us to be. Shame has nothing to do with God. And yet, many people suffer with low self-esteem. That is, a sense of being less-than, an imposter, a feeling that others are better than them – a deep sense of shame. This can create undue social anxiety and depression, resulting in an unfounded need to impress others ... a need to dress the right way, drive the right car, wear the right clothes, or say the right things.

Any time you are tempted to feel ashamed, don't forget where shame came from. It was the first emotion that followed death in the Garden. Again, the true source of shame is death. But God is Life.

Contributing Writer | Sheila Ninowski

## *Action, Application, Accountability*

Decide right now to rid yourself of shame and stop aligning with the devil about who he says you are. Agree with God instead. Know that you are fearfully and wonderfully made, and you have gifts and callings that are without repentance. Dear friend, you're not naked at all. In fact, as a follower of Christ, you are clothed in righteousness, and destined to do mighty exploits for His kingdom. Now go forth and conquer.

# FINDING STRENGTH IN
# THE MIDST OF A STORM

*Jesus made the disciples get into the boat and
go on ahead of Him to the other side, while He
dismissed the crowd. Matthew 14:22*

A sizable crowd followed Jesus to a remote place where He went to pray. He learned that Herod had committed an atrocity and beheaded John the Baptist. Instead of finding solace with God, Jesus was surrounded by throngs of people who were hungry, hurting and in need of a miracle. In spite of His own need, Jesus took time to look on their physical and spiritual hunger. He gave thanks to God for the five loaves of bread and two fish the disciples brought with them, and He miraculously fed over 5,000 men, plus women and children. By His miracles, He revealed Himself as The Messiah, the very Son of God, to those who had hearts to see and to seek God.

"After He had dismissed the crowd, He went up into the hills by Himself to pray. When evening came, He was there alone, but the boat was already a considerable distance from land, buffeted by the waves because the wind was against it." Matthew 14:23. The disciples were huddled in the boat while the winds and storm raged, stirring the waves. Miraculously Jesus walked on water to His disciples. The twelve disciples were terrified they were seeing a ghost. Jesus saw their fears and called to them to have courage, "It is I, do not be afraid."

One responded in faith saying, "Lord if it is you, command me to come to you on the water." It was Peter. And the Lord said, "Come." Eleven disciples stayed in the boat, and one walked on water to go to Jesus.

What would you do? Huddle in the boat or get out of the boat and walk on water to Jesus? What storm are you in or foresee coming your way? Will you seek the Lord with all your heart? Will you take courage, trusting that the Lord's presence, goodness and favor are with you? Will you surrender your will and ask God to replace the desires of your heart with His desires?

His power, strength, and courage are available to us through the Holy Spirit. We can do all things through Christ our Lord who strengthens us.

Contributing Writer | Pat Gordon

## *Action, Application, Accountability*

Have you ever been surrounded by people with needs, when all the while you felt depleted and needed solace with the Lord? Do you recall how Jesus responded? He had compassion and provided His care and healing for their sick bodies and souls. Will you step out in faith as God leads, look with compassion on those who are hurting, and demonstrate both compassion and courage?

# Living in My Own Shadow

*We demolish arguments and every pretension that sets itself up against the knowledge of God, and we take captive every thought to make it obedient to Christ. 2 Corinthians 10:5*

This journey called life ... can catch us by surprise. Sometimes we forget how unique and special God made us. I forgot this truth for a short time. A woman named Sue* played a big part in the lives of people I love, and I worried that I was living in her shadow. Did they see me as her replacement?

To get to the root of emotions, I learned to go back to my childhood. When did I feel I was living in someone's shadow? Perhaps it was with my older sister who took up so much space in our family's lives, not in a positive way. Perhaps it was those who never accepted me, as I was often the "new kid" in town. In my search, I heard someone say, "Unless you believe how special you are, you cannot truly reflect your full light in the world." It was in that moment God spoke to me, "You have only been living in the shadow of who I meant you to be ... until now. You are who I created you to be in this world and you are not living in the shadow of anyone else. Embrace the you I created and shine your light."

Contributing Writer | Vanda Tougas

## *Action, Application, Accountability*

Do you ever feel like you are living in someone's shadow? Could that shadow be the you God intended you to be? Do you want to be free of the worries and fears that hinder your spiritual journey? It's worth the soul-searching to discover what's holding you back, work through that fear and doubt, and trust God's unique and special design of you.

*Not her real name.

# CHANGE IS COMING YOUR WAY

*And we, who with unveiled faces all reflect the Lord's glory, are being transformed into his likeness with ever-increasing glory, which comes from the Lord, who is the Spirit. 2 Corinthians 3:18*

S tatistics say if a person does not accept Christ by the time they are 19 years old, the chance of them ever receiving Christ drops to 10 percent. Why? Because most adults don't want to change. We enjoy where we are and don't realize the need to transform. We enjoy pleasures, self-satisfaction, and our own philosophies about life. Most of us think of self first and others last.

Additionally, most adults are not open to new opinions or ideas, especially about God. Even those in church who envy the peace that believers have are unwilling to change in order to receive it. We don't want to do the work of self-discovery involved for the change to come. Instead, we want a quick fix.

Why? Because we have not had a love affair with Jesus, the King of Kings. We don't know what it means to be changed into His image. God must be sought. His revelations only come by spending time with the Holy Spirit and allowing Him to bring about change and transformation. Though God's mercies are new every morning, His mysteries are only revealed as we spend time in His presence.

Do you need change? How mature is your spiritual walk? Your response to life's tests determines your level of maturity in Christ. How do you respond when you are offended or neglected? Do you gossip or seek revenge? Scripture says we are to love our enemies and do good to those who hate us, to bless those who curse us, and to pray for those who abuse us.

If you are a believer, change is for you. God needs you to be more like Him because we have a world to win. He wants to mend your brokenness. We are all broken people who desperately need His help. Open yourself and look inside. You may not like what you see at first, but I guarantee you, when you allow Him to tweak you, the outcome is incredible, more than you could ask for. For you see, you will become more like Him. Isn't that the reason we are on planet earth to begin with? To be like Him and allow Him to use us? Here's a pearl of wisdom for you: He will bring change one way or the other, so inviting him to do the work is much easier.

Contributing Writer | Liz Morris

## *Action, Application, Accountability*

Open your heart. Let the Savior of the world be your rescue so you can enter His glory on earth. How do you open your heart? Be teachable. Seek wisdom from those who know you best. Are there areas in your life that are blind spots or where pride dictates your actions? Invite the Holy Spirit to reveal dark and wounded places within your heart that He wants to heal. Then allow Him to teach and lead you in His ways rather than the way of pride and selfishness.

# ARE YOU PUZZLED?

*Being confident of this, that He who began a*
*good work in you will carry it on to completion until*
*the day of Christ Jesus. Philippians 1:6*

Before my father passed away, one of his favorite pastimes was working puzzles. He was a master at it, working hours to complete each one. On occasion, I remember engaging in the activity with dad, sorting through the pretty colors and shapes, and organizing them into categories to make assembly more efficient. I remember him stepping back and observing his progress, appreciating the time, patience, and effort that went into placing each piece.

After it was finished, dad carefully disconnected the puzzle in large sections and placed it back into the box with layers of paper separating the sections. Occasionally he would have some of the completed works framed for display, as they were truly beautiful pictures. He had so many puzzles, both completed and waiting to be conquered, he kept them in an outdoor storage unit.

Puzzles can be puzzling, pun intended. Fitting the pieces together can be challenging. The most important piece seems to be the final one that ties it all together. How frustrating to get to the end of a puzzle and discover a piece is missing. It makes the puzzle worker feel their effort has been in vain because the project is left incomplete.

Reflecting on my father and this memory reminds me about the different aspects of my life, from family, friends and acquaintances to ministry, health and the future. My life is an abundance of details that God orchestrates and purposefully fits into place, arranging each piece perfectly by His Will and for His glory. As the verse above reminds us, He who began a good work in us will carry it on to completion until the day of Christ Jesus.

I am thankful that the most important piece of my life's puzzle has been put in place. It is the piece that makes the difference between death and eternal life. John 3:16 says, "For God so loved the world that He gave His only Son, that whoever believes in Him shall not perish but have eternal life."

Have you accepted and received what Jesus did for you on the cross? Unlike the missing pieces of a puzzle, God is easily found. He is just a prayer away. I encourage you, if you haven't already done so, ask Jesus into your life. You will be forever changed into a masterpiece - a completed work of Heart.

Contributing Writer | Jackie Kenney

## *Action, Application, Accountability*

Thank the Father for the memories that remind you of how He is always at work in your life. Give each area of your life to Him daily because His ways are always best.

When you fit the pieces of your life together each morning, be sure part of your preparation and wardrobe is a smile. Your face telegraphs your outlook toward life, toward others and about yourself. Your countenance creates an atmosphere that attracts people toward you or causes them to move away from you. When you smile first, you have decided the direction the relationship will go. Remember, people will follow those who make them feel special, wanted and endeared.

# SAY CHEESE!

*Be joyful always, pray continually, give thanks, for this is God's will for you in Christ Jesus.  1 Thessalonians 5:16-18*

When we take a photo, we say "cheese" to help someone put on a good smile. Sometimes that works and the photo is great. Other times the feelings behind the smile get the best of us, and our not-so-good feelings are portrayed in the photo.

Below are tips for happy pictures or more accurately, tips for feeling happy. God sees us as beautiful, without sin or mistakes. He loves us regardless. How can we reflect more of this happiness?

1.  Be grateful, thanking God for at least one thing each day.
2.  We can discern our feeling or emotion. Is it one of divine approval? Is it peaceful? Or is it a heavy, nagging feeling? If the feeling or emotion is negative, we can rebuke the enemy and turn our thoughts toward Jesus.
3.  Remember, life isn't always a bowl of cherries. We have tribulations now and then. That's our reality since Adam and Eve sinned in the garden. But that's also when we see God working in our lives, when we turn to Him in prayer, read the Bible, and receive help from other Christians. It's when we grow stronger in our faith.
4.  Smile and think about Jesus and you will eventually feel it.

5. Focus on Jesus rather than hurts and disappointments. Jesus said, "I am the Bread of life." He can fill us like nothing else. He is everything. He is the answer.

6. If going down a dark hole, halt and get out of there quickly. It may be the evil one working, so rise above it. Don't let the evil one win. And ask for help when needed.

7. "Act as if". This means we can 'act as if' we are happy or pleased about the situation. This attitude doesn't change the situation, but it changes our focus.

8. Smile and think about Jesus and you will eventually feel it.

9. Be positive in words and actions.

10. Lift others in words and with a smile.

11. Think about serving others. We can ask Jesus to show us someone who needs encouragement and listen for His answer. When we try it we will all be blessed.

The way we see our pictures a year from now is the way God sees us today. He doesn't see the frowns, the closed eyes or the pouts. He sees us as His loving, beautiful creation.

Contributing Writer | Joann Hill

## *Action, Application, Accountability*

Read the tips for feeling happy and consciously live those out today. You will be blessed at the response you get from others as you walk in the joy of being a child of God.

# THE LESSON OF THE WOLF-DOG

*So do not fear, for I am with you. Do not be dismayed, for*
*I am your God. I will strengthen you and help you. I will*
*hold you up with my victorious right hand. Isaiah 41:10*

During the summer, I take long walks in the morning before it gets too warm. On the path, I pass other people walking, running, riding bikes, and walking their dogs. In most areas, there are houses on each side, some with fences and some without.

One morning, I decided to go a little farther through a section that didn't have fences. As I proceeded, I looked to my right and noticed what looked like a wolf, standing on a porch and staring at me. Fear arose so I turned and started back home. After that encounter, I walked to the end of the street and turned around, not crossing the street for fear I would see the creature again. One day I noticed a woman coming towards me, walking two dogs. One looked like the 'wolf' that kept me from moving along the path.

After realizing the 'wolf' was a dog, I continued my walks. Without hesitation, I walked by the house where I noticed the dog before, not looking in that direction. I kept my eyes forward, enjoying the scenery and beauty of God's creation.

I once heard a definition of fear being, "False Evidence Appearing Real." I allowed fear of what I thought was real to keep me from moving forward. It paralyzed me. And that's what fear does when we let it. When

I look back over my life, there have been many times I allowed fear of the unknown, fear of failure, or fear of what others would say, to keep me paralyzed, turning and going back the other way. When I wonder why I wasn't more productive in the Kingdom, I realize I allowed fear to paralyze me instead of faith in God to propel me.

I will remember that summer experience because it was real and relevant. I call it, *The Lesson of The Wolf-Dog*. We are wise to face our fears; they're probably not what we think they are.

Contributing Writer | Lorice E. Perry

## Action, Application, Accountability

Do you have situations in your life where False Evidence Appears Real and causes fear to limit your progress? Ask God to reveal these fears to you so you can surrender them to Him and walk in boldness. Pray, "Father, You tell us not to fear, because You are with us. Help me trust You and Your Word, beyond what I see, so I can walk by faith in victory. Amen."

# CASTING DOWN FEAR

*For God did not give us a spirit of timidity, but a spirit of power, of love and of self-discipline. 2 Timothy 1:7*

A re you struggling to find peace, self-worth, joy or happiness? There have been times in my life where all I felt was fear, and it was horrible. I bought into lies of the enemy and he had me bound. There wasn't a devotional or sermon that told me how to get free. I found sermons on fear, but they were about the fear of failure, public speaking, or heights. There was nothing on the panic-type of fear that can overtake you when you feel as though you are losing your mind.

Many times, I studied, prayed, and fasted for several days. Nothing. I had people lay hands on me and pray. Peace would come for a while. Then, bang. Panic returned to the utmost. Those who have never experienced this type of fear cannot understand the torment. I eventually came to understand that fear is a demonic spirit, sent straight from the pit of hell to destroy life. And I learned that fear has no right to stay after I understood who I am in Christ.

Satan has no legal ground other than the ground we give him. Satan was defeated at the cross. Not only was he defeated, but Jesus disarmed him and made a public spectacle of him, parading him around in his defeat. When He disarmed the rulers and authorities, He made a public display of them, having triumphed over them through Him. Colossians 2:15

We are a new creature. The old man is gone, and our sin was nailed to a tree . . . past, present and future. We can grab hold of our new identity and send the devil back to his home. We no longer have to be bound by fear, depression, anxiety or hopelessness. Jesus' perfect love casts out all fear. Our weapon is to start perfecting ourselves in the love of Christ for others and believing what is ours. And then know, whom the Son sets free is free indeed.

Contributing Writer | Liz Morris

## *Action, Application, Accountability*

If you do not know who you are created to be, and if you don't know Satan is defeated, you believe a lie. Discover grace. If you stay bound in the ministry of death, which is the law, then Satan has a hold on your beliefs. You must believe he has no legal right to your life. Tell him to go.

# BE STILL

*Be still and know that I am God. Psalm 46:10*

I am the youngest of four girls who grew up in a Christian home in the middle of the Bible belt in the 1960's and 1970's. As a seven-year-old, I remember sitting next to my mother in church one Sunday evening. I was bored and fidgeting, so I turned in my seat and stared at the teenagers in the back. I picked up a hymnal and loudly snapped it closed. Then, I got the warning. My mother squeezed my leg just above my knee, gently but firmly. This held me still for approximately one minute.

Fidgeting again, I picked up my Bible and opened it on my lap. As I looked down, these words stood out from the rest, like a pen light had been placed directly above them. *Be still.* Not only was my mother reprimanding me, but God Himself was. I sat still for the remainder of the service. I have carried this scripture in my heart since then.

Years later I learned to apply the rest of the scripture... *and know that I am God.* I am not God. God is God. I don't have all the answers. I don't have to carry the weight of the world on my shoulders. I can rest, rely on, be still, and have confidence that He is God. God has it covered. The creator of the universe, the creator of my humanity, has it covered. All of it. Life. Past, present, and future.

I had to "be still and know that He is God" when the most popular girl at school made fun of me in front of the most popular boy; when my 24-year marriage ended in divorce; when two of my sisters died the same summer; when my two male influences, my father and brother-in-law, died; when I did a drug intervention for my son, and when another son told me all the ways I failed him. Of course, I cried a million tears, ground my teeth, and worried. But not for long, because I had the assurance I could face tomorrow when I rested in knowing He is God and I am not. He is a good God, a wise and loving father, a gentle but firm mother, a kind, protective husband, my all in all.

Contributing Writer | Gayla Seymour

## *Action, Application, Accountability*

For those times you struggle to be still before God because you feel overwhelmed, restless and alone, pray this prayer: "God, You hold the stars in the sky and create every beating heart. You know me personally. When I am restless, overwhelmed or alone, You gently squeeze my leg and whisper *Be still. I am God.* Thank You for loving me, holding my hand, protecting me and providing for me. You are awesome and I love You."

# A Different Perspective
# of Nature

*The heavens declare the glory of God; the skies proclaim the
work of his hands. Day after day they pour forth speech;
night after night they display knowledge. Psalm 19:1-2*

My name is Seven, and I am ten years old. There was a time during the summer when I felt less connected to God. I had not been spending time with Him. It started before I went to my two-week camp in Branson, Missouri.

Right before I was to leave, I talked to my dad about my situation and asked what he thought I should do. He told me to pray that God would lead me back to Him. I prayed but couldn't seem to find an answer. Little did I know I would find the closeness of God during camp.

A week after arriving, my cabin mates went to the lake on an overnight camping trip. We listened to a devotional as we sat on rocks overlooking the lake. The leader spoke about Jesus walking on the water with Peter. As I thought about the devotional, I heard God say in my heart, "I am with you." I looked and saw the sunset, peeking through the mountains. It was a watercolor sky with the sun reflecting off the lake. It was the most beautiful and magnetic sight I had ever seen. It reminded me that God is with me, day in and day out. He was with me as I sat on the rock by the lake. He was there when I was doubtful. Not only was He there, He even knew what I was going through. It made me think, God created that sunset, and He created you and me. God created everything around us.

Do we thank Him for His wonderful works in nature? Do we thank him for his unconditional love? He loves us enough to paint the sky the brightest colors; He loves everyone more than we can imagine.

That night, God showed me that no matter how great the circumstances, He is bigger, and He will take care of me when I fall short. Now, when I see nature, I don't just see the beauty of it. I think of God's perfect creation, and I thank Him for it. May we not take in worldly perspectives, but may we see the world around us as God sees it.

Contributing Writer | Seven Trogdon

## *Action, Application, Accountability*

Does your busyness distract you from the presence of Jesus? How many days, weeks, months or years has it been since you spent time with Him? How long since you were alone and worshiped Him? The Lord explicitly says if we don't worship Him, the rocks will cry out and take our place. Is a rock taking your place of worshiping the One who formed and created you? Find time to talk to Him, to worship Him. Tell Him how majestic He is. The rewards are tremendous. He will speak to you about your life, children, business, and circumstances. "Jesus answered, I tell you, if these become silent, the stones will cry out." Luke 19:40

# DRAGONFLIES AND PROMISES

*I waited patiently for the Lord; He turned to me and heard my cry. He lifted me out of the slimy pit, out of the mud and mire; He set my feet on a rock and gave me a firm place to stand. Psalm 40:1-2*

At the Dallas Zoo, my sons discovered a trading post where they could gather items from nature and trade their collection for one donated by other children. They decided to put together an insect collection to trade for cool rocks. One evening before bed, Tyler asked, "Mom, when you're walking in the morning, will you get us some dead bugs?"

Dead bugs and prayer became the focus of my morning walks. Not only was I looking for dead bugs, I was also looking for confirmation from God that He was real and knew me personally. After a few weeks, we had enough butterflies and bugs for the collection, but no word or indication from God that answered my desperate search for significance. The sons and I attached butterflies and bugs to a foam board and discovered the need for one more dead insect. The perfect space for a dragonfly.

As I headed into my morning walk, I prayed. "Lord, if You love me, if You are real, if You truly have plans for my life, would You give me a dead dragonfly for this insect collection?" Silence. The next morning, I repeated the prayer, out loud, and searched with great expectation.

Again, silence. Not only were there no dead dragonflies, I had not seen one in flight. The absence of dragonflies was peculiar for a Texas summer day, as they were typically plentiful in the warmest months. My asking and God's silence were becoming the new norm, and I was growing frustrated. I had a mission from the sons and was not ready to give up.

On the third day, I pressed into the Lord again. My stubbornness was in the process of metamorphosing into perseverance as I realized the discovery of a dragonfly was no longer the issue. My life seemed to hang in the balance of finding a dragonfly to confirm God's love, purpose, and plan. I cried, "Lord, I need to know you are real."

On this morning walk, my vision was blurred by tears, and my head hung low. As a sprinkler system started, I stepped off the sidewalk, and there, on the side of the road braced against the curb, was a dragonfly. I gently gathered the dead insect and placed it into a zip lock bag. I held my head high and whispered, "thank you" to the heavens. My God was with me. He saw me, He knew me. I was treasured. I was forgiven and loved. He had a plan and purpose for my life.

My silent God waited three days to respond so I would know it was His answer and not coincidence. He used those three days to show me what I valued and who He valued. He gave me the opportunity to lean into Him with expectation of His answer and affirmation of His love. He did all of this through two little boys who wanted to trade dead bugs and butterflies for a rock collection. He indeed set my feet in a safe place; He put a new song in my mouth.

Contributing Writer | Mary Ethel Eckard
Taken from her book, *The Making of a Dragonfly,*
*Following Christ Through the Winds of Change*

## *Action, Application, Accountability*

Waiting on the Lord to rescue and fulfill His promises can test and stretch our faith; even cause us to wonder if He hears or even cares. Oftentimes, he waits to answer our cry so our faith may be stretched. If you are waiting on the Lord, do not lose hope. Continue to seek Him, leaning into His promise, "When you seek me with all your heart, I will be found by you." Jeremiah 29:13

# CAST LOVE

*By this all men will know that you are my disciples,*
*if you love one another. John 13:35*

The Lord offered me an unforgettable love lesson on an Alaskan fishing excursion. My husband, Joe, and I were based out of a fishing lodge with ten other anglers. Each day we went fishing in teams of two or three and reassembled in the evening for dinner and "fish tales." One angler, Jim, spent each evening sullen and complaining, making the seat next to him the least coveted chair at the table.

Toward the end of our trip, while waiting to be picked up from the stream, an ugly comment about Jim escaped my mouth. Joe gave me one of those looks that said, "Why did you say that?" The Holy Spirit added, "Amen!" Instead of being contrite, I blurted out, "Well, it's true!"

After dinner, the head guide came to give us our fishing assignments for the next morning. Jim was assigned as the fishing partner to Joe and me. On returning to our room, instead of feeling remorse, I was angry with the Lord for "punishing me." I determined that the following day I would show Him how nice I could be towards Jim.

The next morning what I began in defiance, God flipped around by filling the situation with His grace through the Holy Spirit. Jim couldn't have been nicer. He helped me in and out of the float plane, escorted me in crossing streams and was attentive to my needs while Joe and the guide were downstream. I learned that he lost his wife of many years several months earlier. He was alone on their planned fishing trip around the world. He missed her. And the opportunity to visit with and assist a woman provided a salve for his hurting heart. That evening, he was a different dinner guest.

I felt ashamed, but the Holy Spirit, so forgiving in God's grace, coached me. He said that Jesus sent me to fish in the world for hurting and lonely people like Jim. And because Jesus is so generous, He gives me His abundant love as bait. My responsibility is to use it.

Contributing Writer | Carolyn Purdy

## *Action, Application, Accountability*

Where is your special calling to cast the love of Christ? In your family? Your neighborhood? Your community? Your city? The world? This bait never runs out, so cast away!

# A New Decade to Speak

*Sing to the Lord a new song; sing to the Lord, all the earth.*
*Sing to the Lord, praise his name; proclaim his salvation*
*day after day. Declare his glory among the nations, his*
*marvelous deeds among all peoples. Psalms 96: 1-3*

As we prepared to enter a new decade, we asked "Lord, what's next?" The Hebrew letter conjoined to the last decade (2010-2019) was "*Ayin*". The letter *Ayin* is the picture symbol of an eye and it represented ten years of seeing the plans God had for us. In the year of 2020 (the Hebrew year 5780) we entered the decade of "*Pey*". The letter *Pey* is the picture symbol of the mouth. God first invited us to see what He was saying and now we are invited to speak what He has shown us. Rise up sons and daughters of praise and shout unto the Lord.

Now is the time to love the Lord and speak of His goodness to all nations. Let's daily give glory to God through prayer and praise. As God calls us beyond our comfort zones, with joy let's be the hands and feet of Jesus and speak abundant life into the dry bones of the lost. May wisdom be the guiding force as we move forward in the Spirit of the Lord and proclaim His good news to the suffering. It is with our mouths we proclaim the authority of Jesus Christ to heal the sick and set the captive free. For whom the Son sets free, he is free indeed.

*Pey* also has the numerical value of 80. Moses was eighty years old when God called him to lead the Israelites from the bondage of Egypt.

We all have a kingdom purpose, no matter what our age. We are never too old to do a new work for the King of Glory. Today, we must know who we are in Christ Jesus and stand on the power he has given us through his death and resurrection, His New Covenant.

*But you are a chosen race, a royal priesthood, a holy nation, a people for his own possession, that you may proclaim the excellencies of him who called you out of darkness into his marvelous light.* 1 Peter 2:9

Are you ready to be His mouthpiece and proclaim the word of faith? Let's say together, Yes and Amen.

*But what does it say? The word is near you, in your mouth and in your heart —that is, the word of faith that we are proclaiming: For if you confess with your mouth that Jesus is Lord and believe in your heart that God raised Him from the dead, you will be saved. For with the heart it is believed for righteousness, and with the mouth it is confessed for salvation.* Romans 10:8-10

Contributing Writer | Stephanie McDaniel

## *Action, Application, Accountability*

What you see determines what you feel. What you hear determines what you speak and do. Put little signs on your refrigerator, mirror or bulletin board to stir your faith. Then go and "speak" His Word with your words and actions. Be God's mouthpiece, hands, and feet to the world around you.

# THE DREADED "D" WORD | DEPRESSION

*God comforts us in every trouble, so that we may also be able to comfort those who are in any kind of trouble or distress, with the comfort with which we ourselves are comforted by God. 2 Corinthians 1:4 (AMPC)*

When life appears pitch black, and we can't see beyond the nose on our face; when days turn into weeks, months, possibly years, what do we as Christians do with it all? What does our Lord have to say? At times the darkness is also eerily silent. Where is He? What is He doing, if anything?

This is a bold, brave writing for me. Why? I have been a born again, spirit-filled, prayer warrior for over three decades. I am also an educated, professional, and loving woman of God. Even still, I have struggled with depression throughout my life. Sadly, the church can regard this affliction as taboo. I couldn't talk about it or admit it for fear of even worse pain and judgment being cast upon me by those who did not understand. Some made me feel that mature and seasoned Christians don't suffer from depression. While well-meaning, these responses only served to wound and eventually alienate me from the very source that should be a strength and comfort, the Body of Christ.

The Lord Jesus Christ does not condemn or rebuke us. He not only understands our deep grief and depression, but He experienced it Himself. In Scripture, we read: "Then they went to a place called Gethsemane, and He said to His disciples, Sit down while I pray. And He took with Him Peter and James and John and began to be struck with terror and amazement and deeply *troubled* and *depressed*. And He said to them, My soul is exceedingly sad (overwhelmed with grief) so that it almost kills Me. Remain here and keep awake and be watching." (Mark 14:32-34 AMPC)

What one needs during these difficult, painful seasons is God's love. He does not deal out shame upon the depressed, but passion. Know that the "Kingdom of God is ... righteousness, peace and joy in the Holy Spirit." (Romans 14:17) We hear that walking in the Spirit, living within our covenant rights, and ascending to the dimension where we are seated next to the Father in Christ, should completely free us from the "D" word. Yes, it can. When we know the truth, it sets us free. We stand on God's promises and we cleave to our Savior.

However, we are on a *journey*, precious ones. Our lives are hidden in Him. We live in grace. We grow. We learn. We go from glory to glory as our faithful, wonderful, perfectly loving Lord brings us through each trial. And as He does, we authentically turn and comfort others with the same comfort with which we ourselves have been comforted. We transform. We become like Christ.

He makes all things work together for good as we pray in the spirit and cleave to Him. This, beautiful souls, may be the very reason it is allowed. These things are not ordained, given, or initiated by our loving Father, but they are allowed. There is a dramatic difference. Trust Him. He holds you. He will never let go. He has a tremendous plan for you, a calling. You are deeply, immutably, and forever loved. You are powerful and effective. This world needs you. The Body of Christ needs you.

Contributing Writer | Linda Churchwell

## *Action, Application, Accountability*

Can God miraculously and instantly heal and remove us from this or any challenging journey? Of course, He can and will, in His time. Stand. Rest. Listen. Seek. Stay the course. If you've suffered in this way or in any other affliction that does not instantaneously leave when rebuked, surrender to the season, the journey, but *not* the affliction. Stay the course.

# INTO THE LIGHT

*But you are a chosen people, a royal priesthood,*
*a holy nation, a people belonging to God, that you*
*may declare the praises of him who called you out of*
*darkness into his wonderful light. 1 Peter 2:9*

Through my childhood and teenage years, I didn't believe I was worthy of love. My parents abandoned me, so I thought that meant I was worthless. I didn't believe in myself and I found no reason to thrive.

In my late teens, I met a guy. I felt he loved me because he took his anger out on me. He verbally, physically, and emotionally abused me. Though he was bipolar and a drug addict, I clung to him as if my life depended on it. I would have done anything for him.

When I was 17, I gave birth to a daughter. This was the first time I understood and learned true love. After she was born, I realized there was something wrong in my relationship with the guy. I loved my daughter and did not want her in the abusive environment, but I didn't know how to get out. I didn't have the strength. At 18, I became pregnant with my son. Their father moved us far away from my family.

When it got to the point of understanding the danger we were in, I knew I had to run. I escaped and returned to Dallas. He followed me. I escaped a second time with the help of a friend, returning to my father's home (although he made it clear he didn't want us there.) At seven months pregnant, I managed to find a job as a telemarketer. Still, I was depressed and in a dark place. After delivering my son, the dark place became darker. I felt like a zombie with an evil curse over me, and I couldn't shake it.

One night in my nearly empty apartment, I remembered reading about Jesus when I was fourteen. My brother had been released from juvenile detention and brought a Bible home. It had a colorful cover and looked modern, so I didn't know it was a Bible. I picked it up and started reading. I was surprised to learn there was a God, and a good one, at that. This dark and empty night, I didn't have a Bible, so I prayed. Miraculously, the dark cloud lifted from me. For the first time in a long time, I was able to see daylight. I actually saw the light. That was the day I realized I had "come back power."

Contributing Writer | Carmen Cabrera

## *Action, Application, Accountability*

Whenever darkness hovers over you and you can't rise above it, remember Christ is the Light of the World. Ask Him to shine His light into your darkness and disperse the hold it has over you to heal you physically, emotionally, mentally, and spiritually. Ask the Lord to restore the hope that comes from walking with Him. Surround yourself with people who speak encouragement and love; surround yourself with His promises and truth. God will give you strength to rise above the darkness and will breathe life back into your dry bones.

# CHOOSE PEACE

*Peace I leave with you; my peace I give you. I do not*
*give to you as the world gives. Do not let your hearts*
*be troubled, and do not be afraid. John 14:27*

J esus said He has given us His very own peace. Did you ever stop to
consider that Jesus does not nervously bite His nails as He looks on
the state of this world? The present state of our government does
not disturb Him, nor is He anxious and worried about the problems
you face. He is at peace. He is smiling and confident as He oversees the
affairs of the universe.

In Galatians 5:22, we see that one of the fruits of the spirit is peace.
The Bible teaches that the Holy Spirit abides in us when we make Jesus
the Lord of our lives. If that is so, then the attributes or fruit of the Spirit
must also be present in us. Though we have the fruit of the Spirit when
we are born again, they are in seed form. We must allow them to grow
and develop in us.

Which brings us back to the topic of peace. Jesus said He has given
us His peace, but it is up to us to allow that peace to increase. How? In
John 14, Jesus explained that troubled, fearful, anxious, and agitated
attitudes are the enemies of peace. We can't be fearful and peaceful at
the same time. We must choose.

It is common for people who deal with fear and anxiety to say, "I
can't help it, I'm just the nervous, anxious type. That's my personality."

If we couldn't overcome fear and anxiety, Jesus would not instruct us as He did when He said, "Let not your hearts be troubled, and do not be afraid." The fact is we can choose to control our thoughts and we can meditate on things that are pure, faith-driven, and positive. This is our God-given right.

Satan, of course, sends thoughts we don't initiate. But we can choose whether to mull those things over or cast them out of our mind. We have power over our thoughts. There are many promises in God's Word that teach us about the good things He has in store for His children. We must keep these things priority in our thinking.

Contributing Writer | Gwen Miller

## *Action, Application, Accountability*

If you have been fearful, anxious and troubled, and if you desire to have the peace of God in your life, pray the following prayer out loud: "Jesus, I want your peace to reign in my heart. Thank you for giving me Your Word, which gives me Your peace to hold me steady in a crazy, mixed-up world. Help me be aware of fearful, anxious thoughts before they take root and overtake my mind. Help me choose peaceful thoughts by choosing to think on your promises. Amen."

# FORGIVENESS

*Bear with one each other and forgive whatever grievances you may have against one another. Forgive as the Lord forgave you. Colossians 3:13*

Have you been around someone who holds onto hurts and pains and passes their attitudes and unforgiveness to you? They may listen to untruths from others but refuse to hear your truth?

At one time, I was hurt by someone in the workforce. It was difficult to let go of the pain and hurt, but as I began to see the unforgiveness bottled within them, I started to understand their motives for behavior and speech. I could not remove the pain from them, but I knew God wanted me to learn forgiveness.

Eventually, I started to change my way of thinking. I discovered that I was not the problem. Unforgiveness was only hurting me. I had to let go and start the healing process to forgive the person. I also learned that, if we allow unforgiveness in our heart, a root of bitterness comes in. If the roots of unforgiveness and bitterness are not removed, they invite sickness into the body.

I learned to let go and to stop taking offense from this person's words and behaviors, even though I felt like a target. If we are not careful, we can become our own roadblock in spiritual growth. We must learn to let go of hurts. We will always find others who value us from the inside out.

Whether in the workforce or in daily life, God wants us to forgive and not allow a root of unforgiveness or bitterness to grow in our hearts. He does not want us caught up in what others do to us. We are to pray for and love them. Learning to replace forgiveness with love helps us grow. When others see our change of attitude and heart, it encourages them to change. The key is to forgive.

Contributing Writer | Barbara Baston

## *Action, Application, Accountability*

Do you have unforgiveness or bitterness in your heart toward anyone, whether they are a co-worker, supervisor, friend, family or church member? Ask the Lord to give you a heart of forgiveness toward those who have hurt you, whether intentionally or unintentionally. Take steps in uprooting anything in your heart that is not a divine representation of the character and attributes of Christ.

# Is it the End or the Beginning?

*I know what it is to be in need, and I know what it is to*
*have plenty. I have learned the secret of being content*
*in any and every situation, whether well fed or hungry,*
*whether living in plenty or in want. Philippians 4:12*

Sometimes it seems nothing is *right*, yet everywhere you turn there is a dead end. When we cannot trace God, those are the very times we must trust Him.

You may think, "I earned a college degree but now cannot locate a job. I fasted, prayed, sought God, followed His leading, yet still no breakthrough. My diet was good, overall healthy and yet *this* evil disease was diagnosed. How can this be?"

God never puts anything but good upon us. He is light and there is no darkness in Him. Every good and perfect gift is from Him. His concern is not for our comfort, but to build our character. The heart of the matter is the matter of the heart.

In Philippians 4:12, Paul said he knows what it is to be in need and what it is to have plenty, but he has also learned the secret of being content in every situation.

Perhaps what seems like the end is the very beginning of an intimate walk with the Lord. Perhaps it's an open door created to allow deep humility to develop within our heart; to seek His still small voice; and be still to abide, hear, and go in a totally different direction, so that He may show His signs, miracles, and wonders through you.

Perhaps today is the beginning of an incredible faith walk into a miracle healing, job, or relationship. God is so outrageous in His Love. As we keep our eyes on Him, contentment, peace, and guidance will flow through even the darkest valley leading to rays of sunshine.

Contributing Writer | Cinthia Shuster

## *Action, Application, Accountability*

Ask the Father to give you wisdom, understanding, and revelation to see the secret riches in hidden places that unfold before you. Don't be in a hurry to rush through a difficult situation, task, or circumstance. Lean on Him and let Him hold your hand through it. Watch for the new thing He is doing in and through you.

# THE GOD OF MIRACLES

*God did extraordinary miracles through Paul, so that*
*even handkerchiefs and aprons that had touched him*
*were taken to the sick, and their illnesses were cured*
*and the evil spirits left them. Acts 19:11-12*

I n June 2019, my husband started working on assignment in San
Juan, Puerto Rico. I was scheduled to join him in August for two
weeks, when I received a call that a category one hurricane was
headed toward Puerto Rico. There was a slight possibility it would
reduce to a tropical storm, so I decided to take the risk and go. After
arriving, I stood on the hotel balcony thanking God for the opportunity
to be there. I knew the hurricane was on its way, but I also knew God
could perform a miracle.

Scripture teaches that one of the gifts of the Holy Spirit is the gift
of miracles. I have seen God perform miracles my entire life. Why?
Because I believe and I expect to see them. I listen to His voice and walk
in obedience. Standing there, I heard God say, 'Command it to go.' With
all confidence, I commanded it to leave. Knowing it would not touch
Puerto Rico, I had immediate faith that it was done. As I looked over
the landscape, I had compassion for the people who suffered greatly
under hurricane Maria a few years earlier. Then I heard the Holy Spirit
say, "I love these people." At that moment, God placed in me a genuine
love for the Puerto Rican people, transforming my compassion to love.

You see, He needs someone with faith and the compassion of Jesus to do His work.

The original weather forecast predicted that a tropical storm would hit the south side of the island. We were staying on the north side. After my command, the hurricane was upgraded to a category two and headed expansively over the entire island. With total confidence, I told my husband, Jeff, "It is not going to hit Puerto Rico at all. Some parts may get a little rain, but we are not going to get anything in San Juan. The Lord spoke and I obeyed." I turned my attention to the enemy and said, "Devil, there will not be a hurricane to hit this island and you know it. God is my vindicator and you are a liar."

That evening, hurricane Dorian turned and headed straight for San Juan. It was forecast to hit the following day at 2 p.m., and it was coming in strong. I looked at my husband and said, "Honey, it's not going to hit. The devil just wants me to lose faith. I have to look beyond what I can see in the natural and know this is spiritual." Jeff also has faith to believe God can move mountains. He said, "That's right. However, FEMA is telling us to work from the hotel the next two days because it looks like we are going to get pounded."

The next day, the palm trees did not sway in the wind and the ocean waves were not building. We turned on the television and realized Fox News was reporting from our hotel. I rushed to the lobby and onto the beach where Fox News was broadcasting. I approached them, asked a few questions, and told them "We prayed, and hurricane Dorian will not be hitting San Juan at all, so you can pack up and go home." You can imagine how they looked at me. Later that afternoon, Jeff and I went to the top floor of the hotel and took pictures of the setting sun. Yes, you heard right. The sun came out that afternoon. We did not have one drop of rain and not one branch of a palm tree swayed in the wind. Only the hand of God can hold back the wind and the rain.

Contributing Writer | Liz Morris

## *Action, Application, Accountability*

Do you believe in or expect miracles? Begin today to develop or strengthen your relationship with God. Tell Him what He means to you and ask Him questions. Listen for His voice and then walk in obedience. The life God intended for us is an incredible journey that few experience because they do not believe.

# MORE NUMEROUS THAN
# THE GRAINS OF SAND

*How precious to me are your thoughts, O God! How*
*vast is the sum of them! Were I to count them, they would*
*outnumber the grains of sand. Psalm 139:17–18a*

One day while meditating on this Scripture, the Lord took me in the Spirit and, for a split second, allowed me to experience His thoughts toward me. All around me were His precious (in Hebrew, the word for precious is *yaqar*, which means esteemed, prized, valuable and costly) uncountable thoughts. Had the Spirit of God not been in control, His intense goodness would have infused my entire being.

After the encounter, I considered the fact that God only has esteemed, prized, valuable and costly thoughts toward me, and those thoughts outnumber the grains of sand. Although my natural, rational mind can not comprehend this truth, my Spirit mind received it, and it changed my life. Through the mind of God, through the empowerment of the Holy Spirit, I began to comprehend not only the vastness of the thoughts of my Father toward me, but also the intensity of His love that is embedded in His every thought. Since that encounter, when faced with a circumstance where I am uncertain how to pray, I recall this Scripture and pray that the esteemed, prized, valuable and costly thoughts of God manifest and are revealed in and through the circumstance.

One of my favorite Scriptures is Nahum 1:9(a), "The Lord is good." It is a simple, yet profound description of the Lord's nature, character, and essence. The Hebrew word for "good" is the word *towb* and means pleasant, excellent, beautiful, and kind. It also means welfare, benefit, prosperity, and morally good in the widest sense.

Knowing that the Lord's character, nature and essence is good allows us to understand that His thoughts toward us are only good, because His thoughts are derived from His character and nature. Those thoughts are not based on who we are or what we have done; they are based on who He is. This is a transforming revelation and is the reason His thoughts toward us are only good and pleasant and are more in number than the grains of sand. When these truths penetrate the heart, we are more prone to look at our life through the lenses of the Lord and His good thoughts toward us, rather than through the lenses of shadows, filled with insecurities and fears, doubts and unbelief.

Our Father only has precious thoughts toward us, and those thoughts are more in number than the grains of sand. We can receive His precious thoughts and allow them to go deep into our heart and soul. We can allow them to change our life, perspective and circumstances, and to transform how we see others.

Contributing Writer | Christina L. McCracken, J.D.
Taken from her book, *Divine Restoration,*
*From Counselor to counselor*

## *Action, Application, Accountability*

Take hold of the deep truths found in Psalm 139:17-18(a). Take a moment to meditate on the vastness of the precious thoughts of God toward you, your family, your loved ones, and your enemies. These truths will change your life, the way you pray for yourself and others. They will cause the lies of the enemy to be expelled and snuffed out of your mind. This Scripture is one of the most powerful in extinguishing the lies of the enemy that seek to tarnish your soul. The precious and valuable thoughts of God toward you are your inheritance, they are your healing, they are your restoration, they are your blessed hope.

# GET BACK UP – YOU ARE IN HIS GRIP

*The steps of a good man are ordered by the Lord;*
*and He delights in his way. Though he may fall, he*
*shall not be utterly cast down, for the Lord upholds*
*him with His hand. Psalm 37: 23-24*

We are often reminded how the steps of a good man are ordered of the Lord. This verse is so often quoted to provide assurance that the Lord guides our paths and we can have confidence in His plans. But what happens when, in our humanness, our decisions take us off the Lord's path?

Through my life, when my decisions haven't aligned with the Lord's path, I discovered the second part of this passage. "Though he may fall, he shall not be utterly cast down." Not only have I not been cast down (as some might have predicted), but this scripture promises the Lord upholds me.

What freedom to seek out and find the grace of Jesus after stumbling in faith. This verse is a foundational truth. No matter what we have done, life is a series of forks in the road, and we can always choose the fork that leads to Jesus.

While we may live with consequences from bad decisions, we can always make the next decision to follow Jesus. Or we can take the fork in the road that leads us back to Jesus, where He orders our steps.

Contributing Writer | Elaine Sommerville

## *Action, Application, Accountability*

If you have stumbled or fallen, don't be discouraged. The Lord will keep you from being totally cast down and He will uphold you. Remember, you are always in His grip.

# HEARING HIS VOICE

*Be still and know that I am God. Psalm 46:10*

At 2 a.m. my husband tugged on my shoulder and said, "Honey, wake up, I think I may be having a heart attack." Panic set in, questions flooded my mind, and I prayed, "Lord, show us what to do." Which hospital should we go to? My husband answered, "Take me to Presbyterian Hospital in Dallas where our daughter was born."

We didn't have a cardiologist, so how would we be sure to get the best doctor? The Lord whispered, "Be still and know that I am God. Trust me." The Lord provided a young specialty surgeon who was also a Christian. Before my husband went into the operating room, the surgeon took our hands, asked his operating staff to join us and prayed. He invited the Holy Spirit to be with my husband during the surgery, to protect him and to bring him safely through. Then, the surgeon prayed for God to guide him as he performed the five-hour operation. Such comfort came to us as we realized the surgeon trusted God to bring healing as much as we did. Though the surgery seemed to take forever, I could feel God's comforting presence with me in the waiting room and knew He was also with my husband and the surgical staff in the operating room. My only option was to trust God completely with the outcome.

In the Intensive Care Unit, my husband was in a lot of pain. Nothing seemed to provide relief. I asked, "Lord, what can I do to help him?" I heard the gentle voice of the Lord answer, "Massage his feet and the top of his head." As I moved from foot to foot and then to his head, my husband's face slowly relaxed. He was able to focus on the pleasurable experience of the massage instead of the excruciating pain. Throughout the weeks of convalescence, I sensed the Lord's presence and voice reminding me, "Be still and know that I am God." His words provided peace and comfort and were a constant reminder that I could trust Him to see us through. Blessed be the name of the Lord.

Contributing Writer | Haroldy W. Woods

## *Action, Application, Accountability*

Find a quiet place today to talk to God, then stop talking and listen for His answer. Do not rush Him but allow time to wait on His response. He will answer, in His way and in His timing.

# MY JOURNEY THROUGH
# THE WILDERNESS

*Daughter, your faith has healed you. Go in peace
and be freed from your suffering. Mark 5:34*

I spent time in the wilderness a few years back. I was walking in my will and didn't even realize I was in the desert. I just knew I kept making the same mistakes, expecting different results. Some call that insanity, and it certainly seemed insane. The suffering was hard and painful, and I couldn't understand how to stop the recurring issues or hurt.

At some point, I called out to God, but it seemed He was nowhere to be found. I mistakenly assumed He had grown weary of my repeated issues. Then one day, I heard Him whisper, "How many more times do we need to do this?" I answered, "No more." In that moment, I understood His gentle counsel to lay down my will and come to Him. Like the prodigal son, I returned to my Father.

A year later, as I was sitting in the church parking lot, I cried, "God, I'm so tired. Please help me. I surrendered to Your will, yet I still hurt." I doubted He heard me; I assumed He had given up on me years earlier, just as I had given up on myself.

I went into the church class I was attending and heard the Pastor say, "I don't know why, but I feel I'm supposed to read this scripture."

He read a story about the woman who had been bleeding for 12 years. She touched the cloak of Jesus and immediately her bleeding stopped. Jesus turned to her and said, "Daughter, your faith has healed you. Go in peace and be freed from your suffering." (Mark 5:34) As the Pastor read, tears streamed down my face. I knew God heard me and was speaking to me through these words. His Spirit reassured me He had healed me from my suffering because I reached out to Him and laid my will at His feet. He had been waiting for me to reach out and touch His cloak.

Scripture says we will have troubles in this world, but we will find peace in Christ. This truth came to life as I sat in class that day. As I made the decision to walk out of the wilderness of my will and turn to Him, God gave me peace and released me from suffering. I am thankful for His gentle nudges that call us out of the desert back into His presence.

Contributing Writer | Cindy Hyde

## *Action, Application, Accountability*

Are you following your own plans, asking God to bless you? Or are you walking in God's perfect plan that promises His blessing? Search deep within. The answer to this question will help you realize whether you are camping in the wilderness or living in the abundance God offers.

# WALKING BY FAITH

*For we live by faith, not by sight. 2 Corinthians 5:7*

The faith journey isn't an easy one. Yet, scripture tells us to stay the course, press on, and to walk by faith and not by sight. My faith has been tested many times. In my 20's, I struggled and often failed to stay the course. Years later, I learned the blessings of trusting when sight tries to overwhelm my faith and trust in God.

I know God is with me through the good, the bad, and the ugly. When my son was 15 months old, he became ill, but my faith stayed steady as I knew he would survive. Twelve years later, my mom was diagnosed with cancer, and I knew she would not survive. Walking by faith through her illness was difficult. Why would God take my mom, a selfless woman, from this world? Though I questioned God and didn't get an answer, my faith never wavered. It was tested, yes, but it never wavered. I just kept repeating, "Okay, Allison, stay the course."

I did not know the journey through my mother's cancer and death would include meeting forever friends and also be the way God directed my path forward. Scripture says He makes beauty from ashes. After my mother's death, I founded a nonprofit ministry that provides financial assistance and empowerment to those going through the challenge of cancer. Through this ministry, I help families focus on getting better rather than worrying about the financial strain. The nonprofit is in memory of my beautiful mother. Though she is not on the earth, her legacy and selflessness continue to bless others.

Contributing Writer | Allison Byrd Haley
Founder, Heavenly Mimi

## *Action, Application, Accountability*

My Heavenly Father led me to walk the course in faith. Invite Him into your situation and He will lead you. Wherever you go, He is with you. Faith is what you need today, tomorrow, and forever. May the Lord bless you on your course of faith.

# What God Longs For

*And with that he breathed on them and said,*
*Receive the Holy Spirit. John 20:22*

D o you realize that, as a believer, the spirit of the resurrected Christ lives within you? Do you know He is looking for those who will trust and obey Him?

He longs for you to truly believe. Why? Because for God, miracles are as simple as breathing; they are what He is made of. His ways are so much higher than ours that even the disciples of Jesus had trouble understanding what He taught. The unregenerate man can never grasp who God is because he does not have the spirit of the resurrected Christ, nor will he ever know or possess what we have as believers.

Do we know what God longs for? He longs for us to come to Him as a child so He can show us His kingdom. It is a kingdom that is so atypical, only a child would believe. God simply wants us to believe. He has a story so profound that even the best of illustrators would be confounded trying to draw it. Yet from the beginning of time, the King has yearned to show us His entire kingdom.

It's a kingdom with no end with a king who loves to please His people. He desires that we walk in His authority and cast down evil entities that try to take over His loved ones. He even gave His only Son so we could have complete authority in this Kingdom. We are to rule and reign and have true provision. He wants us to release control and become Holy Spirit driven, empowered and directed. He wants us to learn and follow His ways, so the full impact of our assignment is protected and wielded by His grace.

If we could fully know His ways and presence, then we would fully cooperate with Him in a way that changes the world around us. It would cause a shift in the atmosphere. Now that's intimacy.

Contributing Writer | Liz Morris

## *Action, Application, Accountability:*

Did you know that you manifest the reality of the world you are most aware of? What are you releasing? The reality of your heavenly kingdom, or the reality of the world? Invite the Holy Spirit to increase your kingdom reality. Pray: "God make me more aware of You. Make it my lifelong goal to allow You to lead. Help my belief to skyrocket so when I walk into a room, the atmosphere shifts and people are touched by Your presence. Help me to host You well and to serve others with the compassion of Jesus. You created me to recognize Your presence and to discern good and evil through my senses. Help me turn my affection toward you daily so others can see Your goodness and mercy. Amen."

# LORD, DO I REALLY HAVE TO FORGIVE?

*But if you forgive men when they sin against you, your heavenly Father will also forgive you. But if you do not forgive men their sins, your Father will not forgive your sins. Matthew 6:14-15*

On January 26, 2011, I was in a serious car accident, driving the same route I had taken for 23 years. I was close to the intersection, 30 feet out, when the traffic signal turned green. I took my foot off the brake, and a truck turned in front of me, causing a collision.

When the driver of the truck approached my car, I asked him to call for an ambulance. His friend stayed on the scene, but no one stayed to be my witness. The police officer arrived and, after being loaded into the ambulance, asked me about the circumstances surrounding the accident. I spoke the truth; however, the young man and his friend said I ran a red light. The police report stated I was the one at fault.

I spent the next 13 days in the hospital with so many broken bones, the nurse said they stopped counting. My knee was so badly broken, the doctor said I might never walk again. I had reconstructive knee-surgery and was confined to a wheelchair for three months. At home, I slept in a hospital bed, and my husband was my caregiver. I told the Lord, "This isn't fair." The Holy Spirit reminded me how Jesus suffered and died for me. Did He deserve the cross and the pain He suffered? I had a choice. Would I walk in forgiveness or bitterness?

Where was God through all of this? He spared my life on the day of the accident. Ten women from church volunteered to stay with me while my husband worked. Depression tried to set in, but I called on the name of Jesus, and it had to leave. I lived out Hebrews 11:1 that says, "Now faith is being sure of what we hope for and certain of what we do not see." I walked by faith rather than sight.

I am a walking miracle. I pray for the young man who hit me, and I have forgiven him. I praise God that I lived, and the young man was not hurt. I choose to defeat the devil by walking in love rather than bitterness.

Contributing Writer | Jody Cox

## *Action, Application, Accountability*

Have you been accused of something you didn't do? Are you holding on to pain that was caused by someone else? Do you find bitterness coming out when the pain of this memory returns? Jesus is our example and He said we must forgive. Let it go, release it to Jesus, and choose to walk in peace. You can do it if you walk in the spirit and not in the flesh. Think about what Jesus did for you and meditate on the Word. Pray and do not let your mind dwell on the past.

# STRENGTH IN TIMES OF TROUBLE

*God is our refuge and strength, an ever-present help in trouble. Psalm 46:1*

S ometimes we have trouble remembering the promises of scripture until we apply them to our circumstances. Psalm 46:1 became a reality to me in my early twenties. I will never forget how this single verse ministered to me and gave me peace in my time of need.

After a long day of work, I looked forward to relaxing. As I undressed and turned toward the shower, somehow, I bumped against the ceramic bathroom sink, which was held in place by a ceramic column. The sink collapsed and fell toward the floor, cracking into many pieces as it hit against the front of my leg between the lower leg area and ankle.

When I tried to move, I fell to the floor. There was no feeling in my leg. Confused, I looked down to see what was happening. The broken ceramic had cut deeply into my leg. I saw a release of blood escaping through the wound.

What was I going to do? I couldn't move. I grew up in a Christian home, attended catholic schools, and attended the Assembly of God church several times a week, so I was familiar with the Word of God. But I had never experienced anything like this before. I had no one to call for help. My father was out of town on business, and I knew I would be unable to awaken my mother due to sleep medication prescribed by her physician. The only thing I could do was call on the name of Jesus.

I cried, "Jesus, it's you and me. Jesus, just you and me. Jesus, you are my strength. Jesus, you are my helper. Jesus, it's you and me."

Because of the power in the name of Jesus, I had the strength and understanding to stand on one leg. I was weak due to blood loss, and the pain was setting in. I grabbed a scarf and wrapped it tightly around my leg to stop the bleeding, all the while repeating, "Jesus, it's just you and me." I dressed, grabbed my purse, and hobbled down the stairs on one leg. Once outside, I asked the security guard of this small apartment building in front of our home to call a taxi.

When I arrived at the hospital, the doctor could not believe I was able to walk into the emergency room. He said, "You have lost a lot of blood. The cut was almost to the tendon. Had it gone any deeper, you would have lost your leg." The accident resulted in 32 stitches to my right leg and debilitated me for months. But I supernaturally recovered at home without needing to go into clinics for therapy. Thanks be to God that He really is our strength and our help in times of trouble. Jesus rescued and healed me because I called upon His name.

Contributing Writer | Carmen Warchol

## *Action, Application, Accountability*

Have you accepted the truth that we have authority through the name of Jesus to call down healing? Miracles are ours if we only believe and call on the name of Jesus. He is our refuge and strength, our ever-present help in times of trouble. He is our Great Physician and our Healer. Not only did Jesus take on our sins as He hung on the cross; He also took on our illness and injuries. Do not be afraid to call on Him in your time of need.

# TOUGH STUFF

*Finally, all of you, live in harmony with one*
*another; be sympathetic, love as brothers, be*
*compassionate and humble. 1 Peter 3:8*

A s we talked, I could feel her pain and sense her deep shame. Most of all, I could perceive her fear of being rejected once again. As her mentor, I listened and let her be herself, risking the openness of sharing with someone she barely knew. She trusted me because we had been paired by an organization that helps women affected by trauma and abuse.

I told her, "Your story is valid and unique. When you share, your burdens and fears become less and feel like a weight has lifted." She replied, "Thank you. I have few people in my life who care about me and what I have been through." She told her story with honesty and pain, even though she had moments when her eyes sparkled. She seemed to gain strength as she shared her experiences, almost too difficult to imagine.

Because I have shared my own childhood issues and struggles in appropriate group situations, I have experienced many conversations like this. We have all been affected by trauma or difficult situations, whether we have personally walked through them or we know someone who has. Trauma is perhaps one of the largest mission fields of this century. Through my journey to health, I experienced breakthroughs as well as setbacks.

Breakthrough conversations follow the steps of the key verse from 1 Peter 3:8. We are told to:

<u>Be of one mind</u>. We do this by listening and asking kind, open-ended questions as learners who hear the heart of the speaker. We don't pressure disclosure, but we trust the Holy Spirit to open a safe place between us.

<u>Empathize</u>. Validate the person's story. Be present and engaged, while giving gracious smiles that show care. Staying silent or crying with the person can be powerful.

<u>Love</u>. Love is tangible. I listened to a mom whose daughter had been molested in a church situation. She expressed how nearly no one helped them. No one prayed in the moment or offered to listen. One of the strongest things we can do for someone suffering is to find a tangible need and try to meet it.

<u>Be Tenderhearted.</u> Remember a time when you put yourself in place of someone who was struggling, and you understood what it would feel like to receive care and love. Trust your instincts about healthy ways you would like to be treated in the same situation.

<u>Embrace Humility.</u> In humility, we focus better on someone else's needs and hear what they are saying. Knowing that we are all created in God's image makes it easier to walk alongside someone, sharing in their suffering and being with them in the moment.

Contributing Writer | Terri Rivera

## Action, Application, Accountability

God created each of us uniquely, which means even our healing journeys are special and different. Jesus heals, but we are His instruments in a world where love is needed. I challenge you to have that special listening/open conversation with a friend-in-need, giving them your heart full of Jesus' love, mercy and grace.

# MOTHER TO DAUGHTER

*Love is patient, love is kind. It does not envy, it does not boast, it is not proud, it is not rude, it is not self-seeking, it is not easily angered, it keeps no record of wrongs. 1 Corinthians 13:4-5*

As your mother, my most important job is to convey God's love and as many of His attributes as I can toward you. I think, know and believe you can do anything because God lives within you. You are His image bearer and His Holy Spirit is accessible to you for help in all things. When I ask, "How can I demonstrate more love toward you?", I am asking (and probing), "Are you lacking in any area where you may think you are not whole? Are you lacking peace, grace, mercy, goodness, kindness, patience, strength, comfort, wisdom, rest, beauty, courage, justice, or abundance of anything?"

I am to show you through my behavior and words the attributes of God, Jesus Christ, and the Holy Spirit so you can live out your created purpose. How can I love you? By proclaiming the truth of God over you.

You are loved. "The Lord appeared to us in the past, saying, I have loved you with an everlasting love; I have drawn you with unfailing kindness." Jeremiah 31:3

You are valuable. "Look at the birds of the air; they do not sow or reap or store away in barns, and yet your Heavenly Father feeds them. Are you not much more valuable than they?" Matthew 6:26

<u>You were bought at a high cost</u>. "For God so loved the world that He gave His one and only Son, that whoever believes in Him shall not perish but have eternal life." John 3:16

<u>You are cherished</u>. "How precious to me are your thoughts, O God! How vast is the sum of them! Were I to count them, they would outnumber the grains of sand." Psalm 139:17-18

<u>There is nothing that can separate you from His love</u>. "For I am convinced that neither death nor life, neither angels nor demons, neither the present nor the future, nor any powers, neither height nor depth, nor anything else in all creation, will be able to separate us from the love of God that is in Christ Jesus our Lord." Romans 8:38-39

<u>You are beautiful</u>. "The Lord does not look at the things people look at. People look at the outward appearance, but the Lord looks at the heart." 1 Samuel 16:7

<u>You are created in His image</u>. "God created mankind in His own image, in the image of God He created them; male and female He created them." Genesis 1:27

## *Action, Application, Accountability*

### *A Blessing for Our Children*

As God's chosen people, holy and dearly loved, clothe yourselves with compassion, kindness, humility, gentleness and patience. Forgive as the Lord forgave you. And over all these virtues put on love, which binds them all together in perfect unity. Let the peace of Christ rule in your hearts. And be thankful. Let the message of Christ dwell among you richly as you teach and admonish one another with all wisdom through psalms, hymns, and songs from the Spirit, singing to God with gratitude in your hearts. And whatever you do, whether in word or deed, do it all in the name of the Lord Jesus, giving thanks to God the Father through Him.

Contributing Writer | Marva Hanks to Maya and Milan

# GREATER WORKS

*I have given you authority to trample on snakes*
*and scorpions and to overcome all the power of the*
*enemy; nothing will harm you. Luke 10:19*

J esus said if we truly believe in Him, we will do greater works than He did. Are you doing the things Jesus did? Do you want to? Let's look at a few of those supernatural situations.

A violent storm came when Jesus and the disciples were in a boat. He rebuked the winds and the sea and there was a dead calm. The disciples asked? "Who is this? Even the winds and the waves obey him!" (Mark 4:35-41)

Two blind men approached Jesus and cried, "Have mercy on us." He asked, "Do you believe that I am able to do this?" They answered, "Yes, Lord." Jesus touched their eyes and said, "According to your faith will it be done to you." They received their sight. (Matthew 9:27-31)

Jesus went into the synagogue and saw a man with a shriveled hand. He said to the man, "Stretch out your hand." The man stretched out his hand and it was completely restored. (Mark 3:1-5)

Lazarus had been in the tomb for four days. When Jesus arrived, he said, "Take away the stone." Then He said, "Did I not tell you that if you believed, you would see the glory of God?" So they took away the stone. Jesus called in a loud voice, "Lazarus, come out!" The dead man came out. (John 11:17-37)

Jesus told the twelve disciples, "The Kingdom of heaven is near, cure the sick, raise the dead, cleanse the lepers and cast out demons." He told them to cure every disease and sickness. We are His disciples. We have access to everything Jesus did. We only need to believe.

God is the same yesterday, today and forever. The same power that raised Jesus from the dead now lives in us.

Contributing Writer | Liz Morris

## *Action, Application, Accountability*

Read in your Bible in the books of Matthew, Mark, Luke and John about the miracles of Jesus. Have you embraced the fact that the Lord has given you the authority to overcome the enemy, using the gifts and abilities He puts in you? You are His ambassadors and instruments on this earth. You are His strategy, His plan to accomplish His purpose. Ask God to help your unbelief.

# GOD'S HUMOR | HAVE YOU EXPERIENCED IT?

*He will take great delight in you – he will rejoice*
*over you with singing. Zephaniah 3:17*

God has a sense of humor. If we look closely throughout the Bible, we can detect His subtle humorous side. It is an aspect of His character that can serve to lighten the mood and make us smile. When we stay close to God, we see it occasionally "pop out," much like a rainbow.

One year while spring cleaning, I came across a baby bed stored in the garage. Our son was 10 and I was 40. My older sister had requested to borrow our baby bed for her upcoming grandchild. Made sense, right? Six months later, I called and asked her to return it. Seems I had a totally unexpected "gift" from God. I was pregnant at the age of 41. We have both laughed repeatedly over God's sense of humor in that incident. At that moment, I glimpsed the humorous feeling Sarah and Abraham must have felt in Genesis 21. Through the ups and downs of daily living, God is likely to toss in the unexpected to tickle and delight us. We must pay close attention, or we can potentially miss it.

Fast forward to that unexpected baby ... a girl ... now a college graduate and about to enter the workforce. Like many young adults, she is not sure what she believes about religion. Is she agnostic? Maybe she believes in God, but not in religious institutions? She finds many excuses to avoid going to church with us. Over the past couple of years, I have prayed regularly for God to find a way to draw her closer to Him. Clearly my influence isn't yet working.

Recently she accepted a job offer in Charleston, South Carolina. The job opportunity came "out of the blue." I began to research Charleston and learned it is called the "Holy City" because ... wait for it .... there are more churches per capita than anywhere else in the United States. There it is. God's "wink" to me, letting me know He is already there ... and He's got this. I've seen a few other signs that let me know not to worry. He's "on the case."

Contributing Writer | Rebecca Campbell


## *Action, Application, Accountability*

God wants us to know, although there will be troubles in this life, there can also be joy and fun. Watch carefully ... don't miss God's humor and joy in your life.

# CONVERSATION CIRCLES

*I praise you, for I am fearfully and
wonderfully made. Psalm 139:14*

This journey called life … begins in different ways for each of us. Some start with a family history of addictions, mental illness, or abuse. Even those with a "normal childhood" face hardships.

Mine was the story of an alcoholic parent and the lies I bought into at an early age about myself, (I am not enough), others, (they will never 'get me'), and the world at large, (it is not a safe place). Through adult conversations, I learned what God says. We are His miracle creation, we are to love others because they are figuring themselves out, and the world is not our home - our safety is in Him.

My children and I have "conversation circles" where we share our struggles and pain. These discussions help us recognize the lies of Satan and replace them with the truth of God, and are a part of our journey to healing and wholeness.

Contributing Writer | Vanda Tougas

## Action, Application, Accountability

Do you need to have conversations with those in your life – your parents, siblings, spouse, children, or someone else? Whatever your childhood struggle, know that healing begins with conversations. Talk to God, a wise friend, a pastor, or a professional counselor.

# REFRESH YOUR SPIRIT

*You will seek me and find me when you seek me with all your heart. Jeremiah 29:13*

Everyone has gone through changing seasons, whether in nature or within the inner life. Deep within your spirit, what season are you in? Is it a season of spring, where your spirit is in a time of sunny and vibrant blooming? Perhaps you're in a summer season, feeling dry and struggling with drought. Or maybe you are wresting with an autumn season, a time of constant change and letting go. Perhaps you are in a spiritual winter, a cold time of weariness and loss due to your health, income, roles, or relationships.

I have experienced each of the changing seasons. The most difficult was when both of my adult children were diagnosed with melanoma cancer. Those dark days tested my faith, broke my heart and drained me. I was so depleted after my son's surgery that I lifted my hand to God, as if to hold onto my Lord's hand. And, in my weakness, I sensed the Lord's presence, favor, power, and mercy that sustained our entire family.

I learned to reach out to the Lord years earlier. When I was 19, a friend talked to me about faith. He said that if we both died, he would go to heaven and I would not. I was stunned. I was a nursing student and my entire life was dedicated to helping people. But he explained that nothing we did could earn our way to heaven. He was certain that when he died, he would go to heaven for one reason: he had a personal relationship with God through His son, Jesus.

Those words touched me deeply. I realized I was unsuccessfully trying to fix the empty places inside by myself. I needed a miracle to transform me from a child of sorrow and deep shame, due to alcoholism in my family, to a child of God who trusted in Christ as my Lord and Savior.

We have personal access to the Lord, through prayer, by reading His words to us, by listening to and singing songs of worship, by listening to His Holy Spirit impress His truths on our hearts, and by serving others. All we need is to ask Him. The choice is ours.

Contributing Writer | Pat Gordon

## *Action, Application, Accountability*

Here are 8 C's for being refreshed and renewed within your spirit:

1. God *cares* about you. Read His word to see how much. The book of John is a great place to start.
2. God *calls* you. His son, Jesus, came to make a way for you to have a personal relationship with Him.
3. The Lord invites us to *come* to Him. He offers to refresh us with His presence, peace, strength and purpose.
4. God listens and forgives us when we *confess* our sins.
5. God responds when we have a *contrite* heart, when we are sorry for turning away from Him.
6. When we ask God to forgive our sins, He promises to *cleanse* us.
7. *Commit* to love God with all your heart, mind, soul and strength. He alone is God and deserves the first place of honor.
8. *Connect* the spirit within you with the spirit of God. He is our source of power, truth, peace and hope. Abide in Him.

# Don't Let Pain Diminish Who You Are

*Turn from evil and do good; seek peace
and pursue it. Psalm 34:14*

Since 2017, many celebrated women have gone public regarding famous men who took unfair advantage of them, using their position of power to lure them into inappropriate intimate encounters. In many ways, the *Me Too* movement has had a cleansing effect by calling into account the men (or sometimes women) who have abused those who are at a professional disadvantage. This movement, for the most part, has been good. However, I have also observed a *boomerang* effect, where some women take the step of shaving their head and becoming almost militant in their defiance to stand up for women's rights. Instead of responding, they react and go to extremes to make their point, which often turns into hatred and unforgiveness and causes them to become someone who is less than God created them to be.

In no way would I invalidate these ladies' experiences. They have truly suffered, and as such, they deserve my respect and attention. I honor them for simply surviving and moving forward in their lives, despite the terrible abuse endured. I also recognize that many of their violators have gotten away with much, and in some cases, deserve years in jail for their crimes. My concern is that these women not lose themselves in the battle. The Bible teaches that we are all equal in the eyes of Christ (Galatians 3:28), which is all I need to reassure me of who I am, and Whose I am. This also grounds me not only in truth, but more specifically, the Truth.

It is important that we not allow the trials of life to rob us of who we are. In the case of the "Me Too" movement, women needn't diminish their femininity simply because an offender took advantage of them. God made these women feminine and beautiful by His own design, not by any man's design, so no man (or woman) has the right to take it away. If we allow our painful experiences to remove a legitimate part of us, the part that God made us to be, then the perpetrator continues to victimize us, even after we've removed ourselves from the abuse. Exhibit A are women who purposely shave their heads, dress more masculine, or take on a tough persona simply because they have been hurt and are reacting to their pain.

While it's appropriate, at times, to speak up for what is right and fight for a cause, we must be prayerful and guarded in the causes we take on, and certainly how we go about it. Are we speaking from godly conviction, or from bitterness and unforgiveness? Are we operating from a place of love (as God's word teaches), or a place of anger? Have we lost our God-given persona in the midst of the battle, and in so doing, have we forfeited even more to the enemy than what was already taken?

Are you, yourself, battling through past abuse or rejection? Be sure you don't lose yourself. Move forward toward true and lasting health. Continue to walk, talk and act like the Christian God calls you to be, speaking the truth - but doing it in love. It's hard to remain gracious and caring when we have become lost in our struggle and fear of being taken advantage of again. But this is something we must strive toward. Mental, physical and spiritual wholeness is what we are after, and true healing, once it is complete, usually leaves no remnant of encroachment on its victim.

Yes, women who have been violated can remain feminine. Children who have been abused can grow up to be responsible adults who contribute to society. We, as Christians, can still walk in love, and keep our focus on the purposes of Christ and His kingdom made manifest. We needn't let offenses rule our lives. The Bible tells us the proper responses, even if they are difficult (i.e., pray for those who spitefully use you). When we do the opposite of what our flesh wants, we win in God's kingdom, and we can often trigger a shift in the spirit realm.

Healing is a process, and for some, it takes much longer than others. But no matter how long it takes, healing is a very important part of getting past the pain, and we simply must pursue it. Just be sure your eye is always on the right prize – not the prize of getting even or making a statement with an angry approach. Your goal is to be the healthy, whole Christian that God created you to be, and no part of your persona should be lost in the process. You, most of all, must work toward a positive, functional, and productive life. God wants this and more for you, and you deserve it.

Contributing Writer | Sheila Ninowski

## *Action, Application, Accountability*

The Bible encourages us to "seek peace and pursue it," peace both within ourselves and with others. This should always be the end game. Along the way of peace, we can learn to love people, love ourselves, and operate in God's supernatural miracles through faith, a faith which can only work by love. The Bible holds the answers to every situation in life. At times, it may not be easy to follow, but it is the Way, the Truth, and the Life, and the true umpire of all we say and do.

# It's Not About the Thumb Drive

*Listen and hear my voice; pay attention and hear what I say. Isaiah 28:23*

I have often said "my Mary" and "my Martha" fight each other. Luke chapter 10 holds the story of when Jesus was a guest in the home of these two sisters. Martha was busy making sure all the details of His visit were taken care of, an important task. Mary, on the other hand, took the opportunity to sit and listen to Jesus.

In the time of Mary and Martha, information was recorded by writing on papyrus with a stick, so how does a story about two sisters from long ago, relate to a thumb drive that stores information from a computer?

As I prepared for an important meeting, I realized I needed to purchase a thumb drive to download some documents. It was rush hour in Dallas, not a convenient time to be on the road, and the temperature was hovering around 100 degrees. Reluctantly, I set out to the office supply store a mere two miles from my home. I fully intended to make this trip in twenty minutes or less.

Mission accomplished, I sat at my computer and plugged in the thumb drive. Immediately it began rapidly flashing. This had never happened before. I was accustomed to the rhythmic flash when downloading information, but this was different. I hurried out in a huff to, once again, face rush hour traffic and return the item. I had important things to do. I did not have time for this interruption.

I approached the service desk. The young man said he had never encountered this problem before and would take a look. He decided it was defective and directed me to pick out a replacement. As he processed the return, I heard in my spirit, "Ask him if he needs prayer." With tears in his eyes, he answered, "Yes Ma'am, for direction."

Normally, wherever I am, I pause to see if the Holy Spirit prompts me to pray for someone. On this day, I was too busy; too focused on what I was doing; too irritated at the interruption, the inconvenience, to listen to what God wanted me to do. That light flashing at me, something that had never happened before, got my attention. It wasn't about the thumb drive; it was about this young man who needed to know God cared about him.

What I was working on was a good thing, a ministry that helps people. But I took my focus off what God most desired, for me to be a light in the darkness wherever I go. This is what He asks of each of us. The world is in turmoil. There are people who need to see Jesus. He asks us not to focus on just doing good works for Him. He simply asks us to reach out and show His love.

Contributing Writer | Sue Arrington

## *Action, Application, Accountability*

Do you struggle with "your Mary" and "your Martha"? When you settle into your quiet time or prayer time with God, is your mind quickly distracted by tasks and to-do lists? Here's a suggestion. As distractions come to mind, list them on paper. This temporarily removes them from your mind and helps you focus on Him. As you focus on Him. He reveals a better way of life. Try it; you may be amazed.

# GOD'S TIMING IS THE RIGHT TIME

*But those who hope in the Lord will renew their strength.
They will soar on wings like eagles; they will run and not
grow weary, they will walk and not be faint. Isaiah 40:31*

We are told in the Bible that God's thoughts and ways are not our thoughts and ways, thank goodness. (And of course, thank God.) We are so often caught up in the daily trees in our lives that we can't step back and see the forest. Yet He can.

One of our most frequent frailties is the one of timing. Whenever we have a problem, we want a solution *now*. If we are sick, we want a pill. If we lose our job, we want another. If our children don't follow our direction, we want immediate behavior modification, etc. Waiting is not in our DNA. And alternatively, sometimes things happen before we are ready.

I was happy and enjoying my job on Madison Avenue in New York City. Retirement was within a reasonable distance. I was having lots of fun embracing the opportunities and energy of "The City." Then of course, it happened. Our company was sold, and the process of internal integration began. Before I knew it, I raised my hand to receive "a package" and within six months I would retire. We made plans to move across country to another state and town near our son and grandbaby. A place we hadn't lived before. It felt abrupt. What would I do besides babysit?

My official retirement date was April 1. On Friday afternoon, April 8, I received a phone call. My older sister had been in a near fatal car accident. The "jaws of life" had taken an hour to extract her from the car, and she was in emergency surgery fighting for her life. Having just moved across country, I was now only a three-hour drive from where she lived, and I was at the hospital before she got out of surgery. I knew the minute I saw her that she was, in fact, my new mission / my new "job."

It wasn't about "me." Timing was perfect for "her." Because I had retired and had no commitments, I spent the next few months at her side, helping her through a very long and difficult recovery and rehabilitation. And through that period, I drew closer to God, drew closer to her, and had ample time to detach and detox from corporate life and plug in to the future.

I would not have chosen this path, but the elegance of the timing can only be God's hand. The next time life does not fit your timetable, look to God and have faith. Trust that He sees something you don't, and the outcome will be one of perfect timing.

Contributing Writer | Rebecca Campbell

## *Action, Application, Accountability*

When it seems you are in seasons of waiting, lean into God and learn to trust Him in all things. Journal your thoughts, emotions, fears and prayers. These will be treasures in the days ahead when hindsight shows you God's activity during the quiet.

# ENEMIES THAT CROWD PASSION

*I consider everything a loss compared to the surpassing greatness of knowing Christ Jesus my Lord, for whose sake I have lost all things. I consider them rubbish, that I may gain Christ and be found in him, not having a righteousness of my own that comes from the law, but that which is through faith in Christ – the righteousness that comes from God and is by faith. I want to know Christ and the power of his resurrection and the fellowship of sharing in his sufferings, becoming like him in his death, and so, somehow, to attain to the resurrection from the dead. Philippians 3:8-11*

Wake up the dreamer within you. Stop looking at where you have been and look at where you are going. Tomorrow is not here yet. Birth it. Seasons change but God's promises to you have not changed. Your miracle is just ahead. Your mind is your world. Get rid of the enemies that crowd out your passion.

If your passion for God's plan has died, pray and ask God to restore it so you can affect the world around you. No one in the Bible ever retired. They kept fulfilling the call because of their passion for Christ. But remember, God made us human beings, not merely human doings. I believe in passionately serving the Lord. But if we emphasize what we do over who we are, we won't be continually growing in the likeness of Christ.

I am thankful God called me to labor together with Him in building a work. But I don't want to become so consumed with the, that I forget Him. I want to be consumed with the Holy Spirit and believe wholeheartedly in the identity and authority that Jesus gave me on this earth.

Paul, probably more than anyone in the Bible, labored with intensity. He poured his heart, soul, and energy into serving the Lord—preaching the gospel, leading people to Christ, planting churches, healing the sick, casting out demons, and discipling young Christians. But he never allowed his passion to take the place of God's presence.

Paul's greatest passion wasn't his work, but his walk with Christ. So, find your God given calling, fulfill it with passion, but keep it balanced with His presence. And when suffering comes, count it all joy because God's grace will sustain you through any trial, temptation or loss you ever experience as long as you are having fellowship and communion with him.

Contributing Writer | Liz Morris

## *Action, Application, Accountability*

Think on these things. Do the things of the world get more of your attention than God? Is making money more important than His assignment for your life? Does what people think concern you more than obeying God's word? Do you spend more time in outside activities than praying and communicating with your Father?

# THIS JOURNEY CALLED LIFE

*Therefore, I tell you, whatever you ask for in prayer, believe that you have received it, and it will be yours. Mark 11:24*

This journey called life is … just too difficult without God. Building a strong and intimate relationship with God requires prayer and worship. I have learned that the power of prayer is equal to the bigness of our belief.

Two years ago, I created a prayer board as a reminder of things and people to consistently pray for, including my family, friends, dreams, and people who need Christ. As I look back, I see how God answered and continues to answer these prayers. The most amazing thing is the string of miracles God has given over the course of time. I am amazed at His faithfulness. All I did was pray. All I did was worship. Things happen in God's timing when our faith is as big as our prayers. We are to pray *big*, believe *big*, and watch Him work our *big* miracle.

Contributing Writer | Vanda Tougas

## *Action, Application, Accountability*

Start a prayer journal to keep track of your prayers and God's answers to your prayers. You, too, will be amazed at His faithfulness. Pray *big*, believe *big*, and expect *big*.

# CHOOSE GOD AND GAIN EVEN MORE

*For whoever has, to him more will be given, and he will have abundance; but whoever does not have, even what he has will be taken away from him. Matthew 13:12 KJV*

I n 1972, Liza Minelli released a song entitled, *God Bless the Child*, co-written by Arthur Herzog, Jr. and Billie Holiday. I first heard this tune when I was a teenager. The lyrics of this song are a mournful lament of the haves and have-nots. This soulful ballad proposes if you are affluent, you'll have lots of friends, but if you lose your wealth, your friends won't stay around. It wasn't until years later I realized the first verse of the song was conceived from Scripture. Unfortunately, this depressing little ballad was an *inaccurate* interpretation of Matthew 13:12. (The world tends to have little ability to interpret the Bible)

In Matthew 13:12, when Jesus made this statement, He meant it to serve as a warning and encouragement for all to follow Him and not reject His teachings. To Jesus, those who heard and responded to Him would grow in grace and character and receive wisdom and godly perception. But those who were too calloused and closed minded would miss their golden opportunity to receive their Messiah's spiritual insight, including salvation. And as a result, even the small bit of spiritual acumen they possessed would be taken from them.

Today, this scripture applies to us, both gentile and Jew. It's similar to the law of habit and use. If a man values something, he pays attention to it and treasures it. If he doesn't, his negligence will cause the thing to wax weaker, degrade, and eventually die. This can apply to both physical and spiritual things. If we ignore the cleaning and maintenance of a house, it will gradually degenerate into disrepair, and one day require demolition. Avoid the necessary hygiene, exercise, diet, and proper care of the body, and it will decline, leading to physical disease and an untimely death. In other words, if we don't cultivate physical objects through careful stewardship, we'll lose what we've been given.

It's no different in the spirit realm. God's objective is that we treasure His Son and the salvation His Son has delivered. In so doing, we tend toward life-building habits, taking care of both our spiritual and physical responsibilities. Life flourishes when we follow God's leading. Death comes when we allow the cares of this world, depression, anger, selfishness or other fleshly deceptions to pull us away from God and His ways.

Contributing Writer | Sheila Ninowski

## *Action, Application, Accountability*

Read Deuteronomy 30:19. Choose this day whom you will serve - either yourself, or your God. Choose Jesus, and He will add to what you have. In so doing, you will gain and not lose, and enjoy a blessed life.

# Where's Our Focus?

*Peter said to him, Aeneas, Jesus Christ heals you. Get up and take care of your mat. Immediately he got up. Acts 9:34*

In Peter's travels, he went to the saints who lived in Lydda where he found Aeneas, a man bedridden and paralyzed for eight years. Peter called him by name, "Aeneas", saying, "Jesus Christ heals you; rise and make your bed."

From the text, we don't know if Aeneas was a Christian. It says Peter went to the saints who lived in Lydda; that's where he found Aeneas. We don't hear him begging or asking Peter for anything. But Peter knew what he needed when he said, "Jesus Christ heals you." It was as if Peter was saying, "Aeneas, Jesus is the one who heals." Was Aeneas seeking his needs in others or was he satisfied in his current state? "Aeneas, Jesus is the answer to your problem; He is your Source."

Are we trusting in God for what we need? Or are we looking to others? Are we satisfied where we are? Where is our faith? When we align our faith with the One who has the power, the provision, the enablement, it forms a channel, a connection to receive what God releases for what we need. Aeneas immediately obeyed the word Peter spoke, "Rise and make your bed." He was healed.

In verse Acts 9:35 we read, "And all the residents of Lydda and Sharon saw him, and they turned to the Lord." Aeneas became a visible testimony to the power of Jesus Christ. And because of his faith, others turned to the Lord. Is our faith in the power of God evident to others?

Contributing Writer | Lorice E. Perry

## *Action, Application, Accountability*

Are you trusting God for what you need or are you looking to others? Is your faith in the power of God evident to others? Do others turn to the Lord because of your Christian walk? Pray, "Father, thank You for being our Source. Open our eyes that we may see You; open our heart that we may believe You and enable us to be a testimony of Your great power. Amen."

# LIVE, LAUGH, AND LOVE

*I tell you, whoever acknowledges me before*
*men, the Son of Man will also acknowledge*
*him before the angels of God. Luke 12:8*

I was alone, face to face with a man from the Middle East. He looked
at me suspiciously, telling me I reminded him of someone he knew.
As he looked deeply into my eyes, he asked me a pointed question.
"Are you Christian?"

His question startled me. We were standing in a hotel lobby in
the Middle East, a country with a strict penalty against anyone who
shared Christ with the Muslim people. In a split second, the possible
consequences of a truthful answer given to the wrong person flooded
my mind. My husband was traveling for business, and I was his travel
companion. My answer could cause us to be immediately expelled from
the country, the business contract could be severed, and/or a $10,000
fine imposed.

The next second, I recalled how the same test of faith had come to
the disciple Peter during the Lord's trial. After denying Christ, he wept
bitterly. Now the test of faith had come to me. There was no doubt in my
mind; the truth had to be spoken. There was no other choice. In my best
attempt to sound pleasant and conversational, I looked into the man's
two penetrating eyes and answered, "Yes, I am."

What came next surprised both me and the man. I sensed a calm and boldness as I shared, "You remind me of someone I know. A Jihadist." The man was shocked and asked, "You know Jihadist?" There and then, the door opened for me to share the truth of how I met a former Jihadist and Muslim, a militant filled with hatred who fought Christians in Lebanon. When this Jihadist had a personal encounter with Jesus, he experienced a miraculous transformation of life, becoming a man of peace with the love of Jesus in his heart.

My new friend listened intently without interruption. He soaked in every word all the while keeping a wary eye out that our conversation was not overheard. I learned his name was Omar. As I finished sharing the story of the transformed Jihadist, a second man appeared, and interrupted our conversation. I could say no more except ask for a business card. As I headed to my room, my heart was burdened for Omar and the people of his country. I could relate to their plight. Years before, I too had been living without hope, without relationship to God the Father and His Son, Jesus.

I was only ready and able to say to Omar, "Yes, I am a Christian," because of one reason. Many years earlier, God performed a miracle when I had an encounter with Jesus Christ that transformed my own life.

Contributing Writer | Pat Gordon

## *Action, Application, Accountability*

Every word you speak is a seed that guarantees a result. Everyone needs reassurance of their worth. Remind yourself throughout the day that each person you meet has encountered waves of criticism, condemnation and inferiority. You can change this. Your words of reassurance can be like water on waves of hope. And as the Holy Spirit leads, share your story of how Jesus Christ has transformed your life which gives you the ability to bring hope to others.

# A Matter of Prayer

*The prayer of a righteous man is powerful*
*and effective. James 5:16*

My son became a believer and accepted Christ in every way an eight-year-old can. His spiritual growth and development at this tender age came from observing other Christians. He witnessed me pray for those who were sick, sad, and suffering emotional pain. When he struggled with life issues, whether school, athletics, or relationships, he came to me for counsel, which usually included a prayer. Modeling prayer and a Christian lifestyle were natural overflows of my love for Christ.

As he grew, he stopped telling me about his hurts and disappointments, as young boys do when they grow into young men. I continued to pray over him as often as he would allow, but our prayer time together decreased as he aged. There were days I struggled with my sons' decisions and attitudes, but I knew without doubt he was God's child. Scripture tells us when we invite Jesus into our hearts, He places His seal (the Holy Spirit) in us, as a guarantee of eternal life.

One morning, I asked God to give me a glimpse into my son's heart, as I sought encouragement that his life was in God's hands. After my son left for school, I hurriedly gathered my belongings for work. A handwritten note on the kitchen counter caught my attention. As I read his scribbled words, tears came to my eyes. "Mom, please pray for my friend. Her house burned last night, and she is scared. They got out of the house safely, but now they are homeless and have lost everything."

My son invited me into his world by asking me to lift his friend to our Heavenly Father. My mama heart was overwhelmed with praise to God for answering my prayer and giving me His reassurance.

Contributing Writer | Mary Ethel Eckard

## Action, Application, Accountability

Your child is worth knowing. Talk. Exchange. Observe. Carefully collect any piece of information that paints a portrait of this "heritage of the Lord." Communicate with the intent to learn rather than condemn. Give your child the nonjudgmental conversation they cannot find anywhere else, and they will keep coming back into your relationship.

# JOHN THE REVELATOR AND GOD'S REVELATION

*Blessed is the one who reads the words of this prophecy,*
*and blessed are those who hear it and take to heart what*
*is written in it, because the time is near. Revelation 1:3*

D id you know, if we read aloud and study the book of Revelation, and if we hear and keep in our hearts what is written, we are promised a blessing? Scripture literally says that. Revelation is a prophecy about Jesus and His return for His people. It is a warning of what is ahead. When He returns, every eye will see Him, even those who pierced Him. And all the tribes of the earth will wail.

For He is the Alpha and the Omega, who was and is and is to come. Revelation says Jesus made us to be a kingdom. As the apostle John was in the spirit, he was told to write a book and send it to the seven churches. Jesus was the one who spoke to him and told him to write what he saw.

John said the voice of Jesus was like the sound of many waters. Try to imagine that. Out of the mouth of Jesus came a two-edged sword, and His face was like the sun shining with full force. Then He spoke, "I am the First and the Last and the Living One." There is only one path to God and that is through his son Jesus. Never compromise this truth.

Jesus said, "I was dead, but now I am alive forever and ever; and I have the keys to death and of hell. Now write John, what you have seen, what is, and what is to take place after this. For the seven stars that you saw, are the seven angels of the seven churches, and the seven lampstands are the seven churches." So, John wrote what he was told about the churches.

We are the church of the last days. We must pay attention to what He said so we don't fall into the things He described about the last days church. These warnings are not about a building; they are about you and me, we are the church. There are promises for the conqueror's, to the ones who overcome, and those promises are unbelievable.

We must be overcomers and not succumb to the world's way of thinking and doing. His desire is that we would not live like the rest of the world in their futile understanding. For they will never get nor understand the wisdom of God because they do not have the Holy Spirit imparting to them. The Bible is foolishness to them. Don't let it become foolishness to you.

Contributing Writer | Liz Morris

## Action, Application, Accountability

God put everything in writing so we could understand His Kingdom and the authority we have. It is important to read and understand the book of Revelation. Be prepared for your life to change and have open ears to hear what the spirit of God speaks as you read.

# MASTER FOCUS

*Let us fix our eyes on Jesus, the author and perfecter of our faith. Hebrews 12:2*

Scottish-American naturalist, author, and environmental philosopher, John Muir, is known as the "Father of the National Parks." One of his famous quotes reads, "In every walk with nature one receives far more than he seeks." This statement resonates within my soul. For most of my adult life, walking outside has functioned not only as my primary means of exercise but also as a great choice for stress relief. These outdoor strolls have offered quiet times of enjoying the beauty of God's world, settling of anxious thoughts, and prayer time with my Heavenly Father. Along the way, I've also encountered sights and sounds which the Holy Spirit has used to encourage my spiritual growth.

On a morning walk along a main street, I noticed a yard maintenance man and his dog. The dog was sitting quietly as the man worked, not wiggling around or distracted by passing cars. She never took her eyes off the worker, remaining seated even as he mowed along the fence, moving farther and farther away from where she was resting. While I watched the man continue his distant mowing, he suddenly, without stopping or turning around, raised his hand and gave a "come" motion. Immediately the dog arose and began to trot towards her master. Her eyes had remained fixed on him, on alert to receive his commands to come and follow.

The observance of this obedient pet caused me to stop and ponder the cacophony of our world, so loud and distracting, and my existence in it. Contemporary life moves at such a fast pace that we often don't make time to sit and rest; our focus zeroed in on our Master. How often does it seem like He must wave, clap, stomp, and even yell to get our attention? In the midst of all the worldly distractions, I want to be more like the faithful dog I observed, having my eyes fixed on Jesus, so that when He quietly gestures, I am ready to move forward in response to His bidding. Do you as well?

Contributing Writer | Carolyn Purdy

## *Action, Application, Accountability*

Take and thank our Lord for quiet walks outside. Enjoy His created beauty in nature. Reflect on how He reveals Himself and the personal relationship He desires with us.

# BE EGGSTRAORDINARY

*All these evils come from inside and make
a man 'unclean.' Mark 7:23*

S ome special recipes call for egg whites. Have you tried to separate
an egg white from the yolk? I have tackled this task many times.
Even when I am extremely careful, and even when I use an egg
separating tool, I manage to get a little of the yolk in the desired egg
white. Then I grab a spoon and scoop out the yolk so my recipe will not
be ruined.

We are much like an egg. Just as the egg has a protective shell, we
have the outer flesh. Just like the egg has liquid parts inside, we have an
inner spirit and a sin nature. Every day we interact with people. When
we encounter less desirable situations with a family member, co-worker,
friend, or any other human, it is sometimes difficult not to get upset,
judgmental, or hold a grudge.

Just like the egg white and the yolk need to be occasionally separated,
we need to separate the person from the sin committed against us. We
need to grasp the fact that the person who wronged us is not that "thing"
or "sin". They are merely the shell with an opposing spirit who has
driven them to sin.

Separation thinking can be difficult to apply, especially if we have
been hurt or wounded deeply. Sometimes it is easier to dump the whole

recipe than it is to scoop out the yellow part. Sometimes it is easier to quit a relationship than it is to walk in love.

Remember, first and foremost, the person who hurt us is our brother or sister in Christ. And the person who sinned against us may be hurting on the inside to act this way. It is their cry for help. Depending on the circumstance, it may take a big spoon to separate, or a big dose of prayer, forgiveness, and grace to walk out the situation. But as we trust God and pray for that individual who wronged us, God will do a mighty work in us and in the other person. God is a faithful God who hears us when we pray and knows us more than we know ourselves.

Contributing Writer | Jackie Kenney

## *Action, Application, Accountability*

The next time you encounter a scrambled situation, try to be "Eggstraordinary" by separating the action from the person God created. Ask God to help you love them unconditionally.

Pray, "Father, thank You that You have given me relationships I can learn from. As I encounter situations with other people that are difficult, give me the grace to walk in love and forgiveness. Amen."

# THE MISSING INGREDIENT

*From him the whole body, joined and held together by
every supporting ligament, grows and builds itself up
in love, as each part does its work. Ephesians 4:16*

My dinner guests arrived right on time, but not me. I dizzily darted about the kitchen running late. Still needing to mix the cornbread, I greeted my friends, served hors d'oeuvres, and excused myself to finish preparations.

Because Mom did not pass along her creative cooking gene, I followed the recipe to the letter. Cornmeal – check. Eggs – got 'em. Milk – double check. Baking powder … where's my baking powder? Dang, I don't have any. Oh, well, it's only ¼ teaspoon. I'll just skip it. I mixed, stirred, poured and popped the pan into the oven. Twenty minutes later I pulled out a sizzling, golden brown, quarter-inch deep cornbread "hockey puck." How could one ingredient in so tiny an amount make such a huge difference?

That's the same question I often asked myself in life. How could my ¼ teaspoon of whatever be enough to make much difference? As a result, I resisted or declined stepping forward whenever I assessed myself as lacking, when I did not count myself as schooled, experienced, positioned, statured, or developed enough to meet the demands of a situation or opportunity.

So, I'll skip it, I thought. Who will notice or miss me? Surely, someone better will step up. More often than not, I saw myself as too little to make a difference. Only later in life, after regrets of missed opportunities and with encouragement from mentors, did I realize my little ¼ teaspoon can make a difference. Where we hear God's call, we can trust He wants us specifically, not someone else, to jump into the mix.

Even when one part stands out more prominently than others, each plays an important role for the best result. No one ingredient is the whole recipe for whatever God is creating at the time. And no unnecessary part exists. Whether we are His one cup of cornmeal, or His two eggs, or His ¼ teaspoon of baking powder, each part matters. We must never underestimate our ¼ teaspoon. Until we get into it, who knows how that too-small-to-count ¼ teaspoon counts in the mix? It may serve as the key catalyst that causes the whole to rise.

Contributing Writer | Gloria Ashby

## *Action, Application, Accountability*

Take an inventory of your gifts and your possessions. Everyone has something to give or plant. Your starting point is anything you have that will benefit another person. Is it your smile, a word of encouragement, time, shared information, money? Your sowing decides your future and greatly enhances the present for those you serve.

# WHO ARE WE TRUSTING?

*But the eyes of the Lord are on those who fear him, on those whose hope is in his unfailing love, to deliver them from death and keep them alive in famine. We wait in hope for the Lord; he is our help and our shield. In him our hearts rejoice, for we trust in his holy name. May your unfailing love rest upon us, O Lord, even as we put our hope in you. Psalms 33:18-22*

When we are looking for someone to trust, we may judge them based on their character, wisdom, strength, faithfulness, ability, and presence. We may ask, "Does this person have a reputable and respectful character? Are they wise in the choices they make? Do they maintain strength for whatever comes against them? Can they be depended on, no matter what? Do they possess ability beyond any other? Can I be assured of their presence when I need them most?"

We might be able to identify a few individuals with some of these attributes, but all in one? Highly unlikely. But there is One who can answer "yes" to all these questions and more. Will we trust Him, the only true and living God, who wants to be Lord of every area of our life? Will we let Him? He's waiting.

Praise the Father for His faithful love toward us. He delivered our soul from death and kept us alive in times of need. He is wise, and we can draw wisdom from Him to make wise choices. Because He is strong, we can lean on Him and be strengthened by Him. Because He is all knowing, we can trust Him to lead us through the circumstances of our life. We can rest in His presence, His provision, His protection, and His peace. We can trust the Father because He is faithful.

Contributing Writer | Lorice E. Perry

## *Action, Application, Accountability*

Our faith and trust in God grow as we release our burdens, situations, and control into His care. When we see how He makes beauty from ashes, our faith grows. Little by little, we see firsthand how all His promises are true. Where are you in your journey of trusting God to handle the small and big details of your life? Today, search your heart. What is your greatest worry or fear? Visualize yourself holding this in the palm of your hand and placing it at the foot of the cross. Ask Jesus to take it from you, to work good from it, and to use it for His glory. Then walk away, knowing He is trustworthy and faithful.

# Our Journey is Made New Everyday

*For we are God's workmanship, created in Christ
Jesus to do good works, which God prepared
in advance for us to do. Ephesians 2:10*

Our past is never meant to be an endless maze that imprisons us, but instead, a portal that opens us to new freedoms - a higher existence. We must remember, however, that the opening of a door often requires the closing of a gate behind us. What you bring through that door is up to you ... so allow yourself to transport only certain things through each portal. Carry the lessons you've learned without bitterness; bring new precepts with you but do so with love and kindness; move forward graciously in forgiveness; and don't forget to pack the catalyst of hope.

Lamentations 3:22-23 says God's compassions are new every day, therefore, so are you. You do have choices. You can live today as a repeat of yesterday, last month, last year, or last decade, or you can live today free and poised for life, your life, filled with the wonder and marvel of who you truly are. And yes, you are a precious marvel of God's handiwork created for a kingdom purpose.

Contributing Writer | Stephanie McDaniel,
Excerpt from her book, *Girl undone, Girl redeemed.*
*Living a legacy of life after trauma*
*(Publication Date: 2020)*

## *Action, Application, Accountability*

There is always more to God. There are different measures and dimensions of His presence. What you do with this insight is up to you. Every believer has an open heaven because you host the presence of God. I pray you begin to live for one thing and one thing alone so your impossible dreams can come true and you can walk in the freedom of the new life rather than the captivity of the past mistakes and burdens.

# HOW SATAN USES BUSYNESS AGAINST YOU

*He who belongs to God hears what God says. The reason you do not hear is that you do not belong to God. John 8:47*

In Luke 10:38-42, we read the story of two sisters, Mary and Martha. Mary sat at the feet of Jesus and listened intently as He spoke. Martha was distracted by tasks and preparations. Jesus said of Mary, "She has chosen what it better, and it will not be taken away from her."

Are you more like Mary or Martha? Even though Jesus used two women to point out Martha's weakness, the lesson applies to everyone. Our lives are filled with busyness and activities that strategically pull us away from spending one-on-one time with our Father.

If we limited the time we talked with our earthly father to once a quarter or once a year, our relationship with him would be limited. It is the same with our heavenly Father. In order to experience the ultimate life on earth, we must carve out time daily to talk to Him. He will tell us things to improve our life, our character and our relationships. He will allow us to see our assignment and our life purpose.

Talking with the Father builds our faith. We can become more intimate with Him than we are with our spouse or best friend. He is closer than our skin; He is inside our heart; He is in our spirit. He knows our frailties and weaknesses. He simply wants to love us and help us become more like Jesus.

One day as I was walking and praying, the Holy Spirit said, "Look up." When I did, I saw where two airplanes had left their smoky mark and created a huge cross in the sky. Then He said, "Look at the width where my arms were nailed. I looked and I could not see the end of the cross on either side." He then said, "That is how much I love you; it is never ending." He invited me to focus on the cross and what it provided for me.

Those intimate moments are life changing, and they are free of charge. Jesus said His sheep hear His voice, but we must be in fellowship with Him, talking to Him and listening for His voice. As believers, we can hear His voice if we will tune in and listen. He desperately wants to talk to each of us. It is our role to stop the enemy from distracting us so we can be like Mary and sit at His feet and listen.

Contributing Writer | Liz Morris

## *Action, Application, Accountability*

To battle against Satan's scheme of busyness, stop right now and talk to God. Then sit, wait and listen. You will discover the best thing on this side of heaven - His voice. Spend time with Him daily.

# IS GOD ON YOUR CALENDAR?

*Do not conform any longer to the pattern of this world
but be transformed by the renewing of your mind. Then
you will be able to test and approve what God's will is –
His good, pleasing and perfect will. Romans 12:2*

I remember opening my calendar, looking at the days ahead, and feeling overwhelmed. I mentioned to my husband, "I have so much to do this week I don't know what to plan for first." My husband wittingly responded, "Let me talk to your scheduler." My husband has a keen sense of humor, but his comment brought me to perspective. I am the one who pencils the events in my calendar.

Sometimes life gets so busy with work, family, volunteering, and social commitments that we feel like we are in a whirlwind. We are so busy doing good things that we forget about the One who is "good all the time." I realized I need to spend more time with the Lord and seek His wisdom and guidance in what He wants me to do and how to handle things.

Our Father in heaven yearns to spend time with His sons and daughters. When we do not spend time in prayer and in His Word, seeking His direction, we find ourselves in a place of confusion and distress. We do not feel His peace that surpasses all understanding.

We have a real enemy who works overtime to keep us distracted. Intentionally scheduling time alone with God keeps us focused on

His plan rather than our own. Going to God first in all we do always turns out for our good. He knows what's best for us in every area of life. We don't know the future, but we know who holds the future. Make your appointment today with Him. He cleared His schedule for you, I promise.

Contributing Writer | Jackie Kenney

## *Action, Application, Accountability*

Let God decide your daily agenda, and your life will take a new direction. One hour with God can easily reveal the fatal flaws in your most carefully laid plans. He who thrives in prayer, thrives. Develop conversations in the presence of God; talking aloud to God creates profound and indescribable results.

# JUST BE | THE HOW

*As water reflects the face, so one's life
reflects the heart.* Proverbs 27:19

A friend recently asked a thought-provoking question: "As a Jesus follower, we are taught to love others, be humble and obedient, and live like Jesus. In today's confused and individualistic culture, it seems most Christians struggle with *how* to do these things. What is love? What is humility? What does it mean to walk with Jesus, and *how* does that look for believers?"

My response provides the guidance I received from the Holy Spirit over a period of years. "The way I live out the Jesus-life is to spend time with Him in scripture, worshiping, and talking with Him. My life passion is to cultivate a deep and abiding love relationship with God."

"What is in the heart naturally overflows into other relationships. The way to love others is to be genuine and authentic yet caring more about obedience to God than pleasing man. When we live for God and don't bow down to the whims of people, He naturally flows through us. He tenders our attitudes, triggers, motives, etc., as we spend time with Him. Too often we are caught up in *how* to behave and talk like a Christian, which is stressful. One day, as I struggled with a failed attempt to love someone, the Lord said, "My child, just be. Be who I created you to be. Love Me, and My love will flow out of you. You will reflect me without even knowing it. That's *how*."

I stopped striving to behave like a Christian and focused on becoming the *me* God created. After all, as my Creator, only He knows my potential, purpose, and true passions, my struggles and inner workings. When He shows me wounds, triggers, hurts, poor attitudes or behaviors, I see them through His eyes of love. He doesn't reveal these things as punishment or conviction, but because He loves and wants me whole. He wants me to fulfill my purpose and reach my destiny. As He peels away the layers of the broken-inner-me, I ask Him to walk me through healing, so my life is a clearer reflection of His character.

The journey becomes abundant when He becomes our focus. As we learn who He is, we love Him more. As we understand how His grace and love toward us are unshakeable, our love and devotion increase. It's as if He injects our heart with a seed of love, and as the seed grows, it becomes a tree that produces love, joy, humility, obedience, peace, etc. This is done with only the effort it takes to abide in Him by spending time with Him. Then, the love we show others is simply and easily an overflow of our love for God.

Though I make it sound easy to 'just be,' I confess it took years to grow comfortable with this process. I wanted to earn God's love and grace so I would feel assured He would never take it away. I realized the fear of rejection was working against God's perfect promise of 'never leaving nor forsaking me.'

For those who have not spent time with God, the cultivation of a love-relationship with Him may be difficult because it takes time and intentionality to build and maintain continual communion with the Holy Spirit. But the payoff is abiding in His goodness, His abundant love and grace.

Contributing Writer | Mary Ethel Eckard

## *Action, Application, Accountability*

Learning to "just be" is a step by step process that can be cultivated in your timeframe without stress, striving, or fear of rejection. Take a first step today. Read Psalm 1 or whisper a prayer. And give yourself grace as you learn to "just be."

# NEVER ALONE

*The Lord himself goes before you and will be with you;*
*he will never leave you nor forsake you. Do not be*
*afraid; do not be discouraged. Deuteronomy 31:8*

It's wonderful how God reaches into our everyday lives and uses ordinary things to get our attention. For me, He used a poem.

I received salvation as a little girl, but when my father died a few years later, my young heart was devastated. As a family, we endured a lot of hardship. I felt alone and abandoned. This led me to the conclusion that God wasn't real or didn't care. I decided I would no longer be a Christian. I let go of God, but He never let go of me.

Years later, I found myself living a fabulous life with my dream job, more money than I thought possible, and an adoring husband. Yet, I felt empty. At night, I would lay in bed and think, "I have such a good life, why am I not happy?" I would hear a voice in my heart respond, "Your life is incomplete because you have not invited me to be part of it."

I knew it was the Holy Spirit speaking to me, but I didn't want to listen. My wounded heart was too afraid. Then one day, the poem *Footprints* came across my desk and I read it for the first time. What a perfect visual those words portrayed. It was as though I could hear the strong, resounding voice of God reading the poem to me, specifically the portion that reads, "It was then that I carried you."

Right then I knew those words were truth. He carried me through my hard days. I rededicated my life to the Lord and regained that third dimension of joy and peace I remembered as a young girl. God is so faithful. Not only did He never leave me nor forsake me, but I am convinced His mantle of protection and blessing continuously surrounded me. He did not stop wooing and pursuing me until I returned to an intimate relationship with Him.

Contributing Writer | Kathleen Watson

## *Action, Application, Accountability*

Find the poem, *Footprints in the Sand* online and read it.

# JOY: A SUPERNATURAL FORCE

*The joy of the Lord is your strength. Nehemiah 8:10*

J oy is more than a warm, happy feeling when things are going our way. It is one of the most powerful spiritual forces available to Christians. In Nehemiah 8:10, we read that joy is strength; the two are interchangeable according to this scripture, which is why joy is so important. We can't have a life of faith without being strong in the Lord. God's recipe for strength is spelled J-O-Y. Joy is not a state of mind or a changing emotion. It is a very real force which the devil is powerless to defeat. Just as fear must yield to faith, discouragement must yield to joy.

Joy is listed in Galatians 5:22 as part of the fruit of the Holy Spirit. That means, as Christians, we have joy within. The Holy Spirit comes to live in us when we receive salvation, and He makes a God-like nature available to us. "Therefore, be imitators of God (copy Him and follow His example,) as well-beloved children (imitate their father)." This passage from Ephesians 5:1 says, as children of God, we are to imitate Him. A godly nature is imparted to us at salvation. By that, we have the amazing opportunity to walk supernaturally.

Though the character and nature of God are deposited in us at salvation, we must develop our character and God's nature in order to live by its power. How do we develop the godly characteristic of joy? We speak God's Word over our life and believe God above our circumstances. When everyone at work gets laid off, we go to God's

Word and find promises for blessing and provision. We speak those words over our life and we make God's Word the final authority in our work situation. We then thank God for what He has promised in His word regarding our life. We make the choice to think on what God says about our life and future. In doing this, the joy of the Lord will begin to roll around on the inside and we will have peace when others are experiencing discouragement and fear.

Joy can be present in our life in the midst of great trouble. There is no greater witness to the power of God in this earth than a person who has unshakable joy and peace. Even with tears streaming down our cheeks and a lump in our throat, we can say, "Lord, I trust you and I am thankful that you provide for me. Whether I see it now, I know you are faithful." That kind of prayer causes change to our situation and that kind of trust is most pleasing to God.

Anyone can have joy when things are going well, but only those who know God and what His Word says can experience joy in the midst of turmoil.

Contributing Writer | Gwen Miller

## *Action, Application, Accountability*

If you are in a time of challenge or hardship, if worries and anxieties try to interfere with your peace and joy, remember the promises of God and pray: "Lord, I trust you and I am thankful that you provide for me. Whether I see it now, I know you are faithful. Amen."

# A Moment at the Well

*Yet a time is coming and has now come when the true worshipers will worship the Father in spirit and truth, for they are the kind of worshipers the Father seeks. John 4:23*

At high noon on a hot and dry day, a woman stops by a well to fill her jar. This is not just any well. It is the well at Sychar, the same well where Jacob met Rachel and experienced love at first sight. (Genesis 29:9-12)

This is a different story of love at first sight. The woman's name is Photine, and she is not thinking about romance. The only thing on her mind is filling her jar without facing the condemnation of her accusers. This ordained meeting on an ordinary day brought her to the feet of Jesus, a man who seemed to know her heart. He saw that, though her jar was empty, she was filled with shame and regret.

How did He know the things she kept hidden? How did He know the things she had done, both in secret and in the open? He had not seen her transgressions, yet He knew them all. This chance encounter with a stranger changed her life, freeing her from the past to pursue a future in Christ.

How many times have you wished your circumstance could be instantly changed? How many times have you longed to be free from the burden of things you hoped no one would ever know; the nagging memories of a darker you? How many days have you thirsted for relief from the dry despair of your circumstance?

In only a moment with the Savior, you can empty your burdens and rejoice as He moves you from a dry place into a pool of redeeming water. Water so refreshing, you can splash and bathe in the freedom only He can give. Each day you can emerge from your time at the Well and move forward, refreshed and filled with new hope. This time alone with Jesus, baring your soul to Him, confessing your transgressions, is no guarantee that your day will be filled with perfect bliss. Photine and her family went on to suffer martyrdom for Christ.

You will fail at times, be drawn into behaviors which are not exemplary, or dire circumstances not of your choosing. But you have the assurance that, at any moment, you can go to the well and call upon Jesus to meet you. You can empty your jar of junk and fill it, once again, with the pure water of hope and forgiveness. Once filled, you can leave the well refreshed and renewed, carrying the love of Christ to a lost and hurting world.

Contributing Writer | Sue Arrington
Taken from her book, *Killin' Snakes, For We Wrestle Not Against Flesh and Blood*

## Action, Application, Accountability

Spend a few moments alone with Jesus, baring your soul to Him, confessing your transgressions. He sees and knows the things you have done, even those things you try to keep hidden. And yet, He extends His love and forgiveness to you so you can be free from the shame and guilt of your past. Take this opportunity to drink in the refreshing water of His presence, allowing Him to replace your burdens with renewed hope.

# NOWHERE I'D RATHER BE

*But whatever was to my profit I now consider loss for the sake of Christ. What is more, I consider everything a loss compared to the surpassing greatness of knowing Christ Jesus my Lord, for whose sake I have lost all things. I consider them rubbish, that I may gain Christ and be found in him. Philippians 3:7-8*

There's nowhere I would rather be than in the presence of the Holy Spirit. It's as if time stands still and I get lost in the mystery of His presence. Oh, the wonder of those moments when He speaks, and when I listen. I never want to leave. I am so found in His love, all I want to do is lift my hands in praise. Sometimes I stand still like a statue and other times, I dance around the room. It's as if the wind blows across my face and He is with me. A perfect dance with the lover of my soul and His simple, open, untethered love. Beneath the surface of my imagination is a calmness I don't feel anywhere else. He is the comforter of my mind, and my spirit soars to new heights.

It's in the waiting. The anticipation we are going to meet; that He is going to ask me something and wait for my answer. Or, I am going to tell Him something and He will respond. The best part is knowing He is already pleased with me and there is nothing for me to prove. I revel in the fact that Jesus paid it all, as it allows neither spot nor blemish to stand between us. I don't worry that He is not pleased with me or that I have done something wrong. Jesus already took care of that. I can come boldly and cleansed before His throne of grace.

Your Father only wants to give you His good pleasure. Don't you want to step into that covenant relationship with Him? God says, "Look to me and be saved!" It's that simple. Then comes the intimacy. But that part is up to you.

Start your moments telling Him everything you are thankful for. Then move into praise, telling Him how majestic and awesome and powerful He is. Move into worshiping Him, which takes you right into His throne room. Then pray in the spirit, as that is prophesying your perfect future. Lastly tell Him your heart's desire.

He's not a system, but He does have characteristics or facets of communion between us and Him that He loves and desires. Always ask for His wisdom, He will grant it.

If your mind starts to wander into creativity and possibilities, that is fine. It's in those sacred moments the Holy Spirit speaks. Write it down and continue. He gives nuggets for life in those moments. Sometimes He gives visions or direction.

This is the intimate part. He loves you so much more than you can comprehend. He has so much for you to accomplish in His Kingdom.

Contributing Writer | Liz Morris

## *Action, Application, Accountability*

Listen to Christian worship songs that bring you into the presence of God. Several powerful ones include: *Where You Are* by Jeremy Riddle,

*Nothing Else* by Cody Carnes, *This is a Move* by Brandon Lake and Tasha Cobbs Leonard, and *Communion* by Brandon Lake and Steffany Gretzinger. You can find others by doing an online search for 'worship songs that bring God's presence.'

# SEE WHAT I AM REALLY MADE OF

*They overcame him by the blood of the Lamb, and by*
*the word of their testimony; they did not love their lives*
*so much as to shrink from death. Revelation 12:11*

S everal years ago, I had an encounter with the Lord. He showed
me His strong right arm and a vial of blood. He asked, "What do
you do with a vial of blood?" I replied, "Test it, to see what is in
the blood." "Exactly," the Lord responded, "I want you to test My blood
to see what I am really made of." I knew I had much to learn about my
Savior's blood. I also knew He was eager to show me what He was really
made of; for who He is - His divine essence - is found in His blood. I
have not mastered this lesson. However, the more I know about the
blood of Christ and His redemption, the more I realize what my glorious
inheritance is as an heir of God in Christ Jesus.

In Ephesians 1:7 the Apostle Paul prayed for us, stating, "in Him we
have redemption through His blood, the forgiveness of sins." Paul had
divine knowledge of the all-encompassing power of Christ's redemption
found in His blood, and he wanted us to experience this power as well.

The word *redemption* used in the verse above is the Greek word
*apolytrosis*. It means a releasing or liberation effected by the payment
of a ransom, or to redeem one by paying the price of a debt. The word
*forgiveness* is the Greek word *aphesis* and means a release from bondage

or imprisonment, to pardon or to let go as if one had never committed the offense.

The blood of Jesus Christ is our emotional, physical and spiritual liberator, the full payment needed for our release from all bondages, all debts and all limitations caused by sin; whether generational, family, corporate, personal or the sins of others. The blood of Jesus Christ not only offers us eternal life through paying the spiritual debt we owe to the Father but is also the final payment required for everything we need to be brought back into 100% alignment with the plans and purposes of God for our lives. Our divine destiny, spiritual inheritance, and eternal glory are found in His blood.

The blood of Jesus is our game changer, it is how we overcome all things. Our personal testimony is embodied in the blood of Jesus. No people group on the face of the earth can testify to the redemption power found in the blood of Jesus other than a born-again, forgiven Christ follower.

The blood of Jesus is our way maker, offering us access before the throne of God. It is the voice of our cry of "mercy over judgment;" it is a divine bulldozer tearing down and rooting up everything in the way to our destiny and purpose. The blood of Jesus is the destroyer of every work of darkness formed in our lives, whether internal or external, known or unknown, seen or unseen. It is our protector, our rock-solid defense; it is our conscience purifier and mind transformer. It is our door of access and the key that opens every lock. It is the voice of authority, overriding all other voices, declaring our victory and our triumph. It is our surety, our pledge, our strength in times of testing and our armor during battle. It is our sure and certain spiritual foundation, our reconciler, our peace, our physical and emotional healing and is the essence of transforming love. It is our perfection, our everlasting covenant, our eternal redemption. It is our divine glory.

Contributing Writer | Christina L. McCracken, J.D.
Taken from her book, *Divine Restoration, From Counselor to counselor*

## *Action, Application, Accountability*

Consider the Lord's challenge. Can you now see why the Lord wants us to know what He is really made of? Do you know what He is really made of? Oh, the blood of Jesus, it washes white as snow.

# LABOR TO REST

*Therefore, since a promise remains of entering
His rest, let us fear lest any of you seem to have
come short of it. Hebrews 4:1 (KJV)*

O ur Father wants us to enter His rest, even as He did on the seventh day after completing His work of creation. Hebrews 4:11 goes on to say: "Let us labor therefore to enter into that rest, lest any man fall after the same example of unbelief." So, if we are to labor to do anything, it is to enter His rest. This "rest" is two-fold.

First, under the new covenant, Jesus completed His work on the cross so we wouldn't have to labor our way into Heaven. To enter that rest, all we must do is accept and believe on Christ (and His completed work). It's difficult for some to accept this beautiful exchange, but it is based upon His grace and our faith in it. It has nothing to do with our works.

Secondly, this passage encourages us to believe and trust God. I must admit, it is difficult to rest. It's easy to trust God when things are smooth sailing but challenging when life becomes chaotic or tragic. The truth is, God urges us to trust Him.

In Hebrews 3, we read that God considered the Jews to be disobedient as they wandered through the wilderness. As a result, most of them were never allowed to enter the promised land, which was their place of hope and rest. How were they disobedient? Exodus tells us they complained

145

and rebelled by building a golden calf to worship. But the writer of Hebrews doesn't emphasize these sinful events. In fact, the single act of disobedience he cites is their unbelief.

In Hebrews 3:8-11, the Holy Spirit quotes Psalms 95: "Today, if you will hear His voice, do not harden your hearts as in the rebellion, in the day of trial in the wilderness, where your fathers tested Me, tried Me, and saw My works forty years. Therefore, I was angry with that generation, and said, they always go astray in their heart, And they have not known My ways. So I swore in My wrath, they shall not enter My rest."

The writer of Hebrews is not speaking about the Israelites' whining, or their blatant rebellious acts. He is associating their sinful hearts with their unbelief. And He finishes the chapter with this: "And to whom did God swear that they would never enter his rest if not to those who disobeyed? So we see that they were not able to enter, because of their unbelief." Hebrews 3:18, 19

What does this say to those of us who are in the new covenant? Since the wilderness experience is cited in Hebrews along with the challenge to enter His rest, the message is the same for us. We must learn from their mistakes. We must work on trusting and believing Him even in the tough times. We must turn toward Him. Daily.

Contributing Writer | Sheila Ninowski

## *Action, Application, Accountability*

Reading the Bible is a must. Faith comes by hearing God's word consistently, so we must grow in belief by feeding upon scripture and spending more intimate time with God. Let's not fall into the trap of disobedience through unbelief. Let us labor to enter His rest.

# NEVER STOP PRAYING

*The Lord is not slow in keeping his promise, as some understand slowness. Instead he is patient with you, not wanting anyone to perish, but everyone to come to repentance. 2 Peter 3:9*

Never stop praying for your loved ones, and never lose hope. Often, we never know what truly transpires between another soul and the Lord, or the true ending of another's story.

The grandmother of my husband, Brad, is a perfect example. Years ago, when Brad first received salvation, he was ecstatic to share his faith with his beloved grandma. She appeared to others to be a hardened woman, a former barkeep, and even a 'Rosie the riveter' in the war. She smoked cigarettes like a chimney, swore like a sailor, and never darkened the door of the church, but she loved her family, especially her grandchildren.

When Brad would tell her about Jesus, she would become irate and, with colorful language, express her desire not to hear it. Brad was so distraught that she would not hear him out, and he feared she might never know Jesus as her own personal Savior. After continual prayer, the Lord led Brad to write his testimony. She might not want to talk about salvation, but maybe she would, in anonymity, listen. So, he mailed it and we prayed. Shortly after, she became ill, went to the hospital, and died. Brad was heartbroken. He didn't know if his grandma had received or read the letter. He was not able to talk or pray with her.

Upon attending grandma's funeral, a nurse from the hospital approached Brad and said, "You're Brad? It's nice to meet you. Isn't it wonderful news about your grandmother?" Brad was shocked and said, "Good news?" The nurse replied, "You haven't heard?" She went on to explain that when his grandma was in the hospital, she went flat line, but the doctors were able to revive her. When they did, she was hysterical, calling for Brad and his letter. Brad's grandpa went back to their house, found the letter and took it to the hospital. When the nurse read it, she knew exactly what happened and why grandma wanted to see Brad. The nurse said that she, too, was a Christian, and she had the opportunity to minister to grandma and lead her in a prayer to give Jesus Christ the Lordship of her life. After grandma's name was written in the "Lamb's Book of Life", she closed her eyes, with a smile on her face, and went flat line again. "Brad," the nurse said, "your grandmother is in heaven."

Had Brad not seen the nurse that day, he would not have known the end of the story of God's mercy and intervention. He would not know of his own answered prayer for his grandma, nor his assurance of her residence in heaven. Never lose hope or faith that God will accomplish His good, pleasing and perfect will. Never stop praying.

Contributing Writer | Kathleen Watson

## *Action, Application, Accountability*

Read 1 Timothy 2:1-4. Never stop witnessing to and praying for those God has placed on your heart. Sometimes we plant the seeds and others harvest, but God provides the increase.

# GOD'S MIGHTY WARRIORS

*For it has been granted to you on behalf of Christ not
only to believe on him, but also to suffer for him, since
you are going through the same struggle you saw I had,
and now hear that I still have. Philippians 1:29-30*

I magine being in the shoes of Abraham, a prominent and affluent
man in his community. God asked him to leave his own land and
move to an unknown country where he would live in a tent. God
promised him a son and, after waiting 25 years for the son to be born,
God asked Abraham to offer his son, Isaac, as a sacrifice on an altar. This
should have been Isaac's death. Do you think Abraham obeyed God?
Yes, he did. But before the sacrifice could be made, God provided a way
out, a ram hidden in the thicket. God tested Abraham's faithfulness.
Why? Because Abraham is the man who received a promise from God
that, through his seed, God would bless the whole world.

Abraham's test was difficult, wasn't it? God knew a child was the
one thing a human could love more than Him. Is this true in your life?
Do you love your children more than you love God? I had to face this
reality years ago, and I had to get to a place where I could honestly say,
"No Lord. I love you the most."

Life is full of surprises. Some surprises are not pleasant, and we find
ourselves fighting situations we never thought we would face. I have
faced several battles that, if not for the Lord, I would have lost. Through

the years, the Lord taught me how to fight. One of our best weapons is worship. When we truly learn to worship in spirit and in truth, the battle is won for us.

Think about the great people of the Bible and their enormous difficulties. Besides Abraham, consider Joshua, David, Gideon, Joseph and Moses. Remember the disciples of Jesus who were persecuted in a multitude of ways. Everyone who desired to live close to God went through great difficulties. Yet, we see over and over how they turned to worshiping God in their battles and how He delivered them because of their belief in Him.

Be encouraged. The greater the test, the greater the victory; the greater the suffering, the greater the blessing. All great men used by God learned to fight in His Kingdom. The moments of great difficulties are the moments the most resounding victories are born.

What tests are you going through today? Be a warrior and trust God to see you through. Be faithful to Him and obey, and your seed, your offspring, your generations to come, will receive the blessings.

Contributing Writer | Liz Morris

## *Action, Application, Accountability*

When going through a test or trial, remember to worship God and turn your focus to Him. Rather than worrying and trying to figure out your move in every situation, trust in God to show you every step and decision. When we truly learn to worship in spirit and in truth, the battle is won for us.

# WHAT IF …

*Do not turn me over to the desire of my foes, for false witnesses rise up against me, breathing out violence. I am still confident of this: I will see the goodness of the Lord in the land of the living. Wait for the Lord; be strong and take heart and wait for the Lord. Psalm 27:12-14*

What if today was the day you woke up and everything you dreamed of suddenly came to pass? The heartache from the husband who didn't follow through and was never there when you needed him, suddenly turned around? The sickness that plagued your loved one for years suddenly was healed. The pain you felt as your child went down a path that was so totally out of line from the one in which you raised them suddenly changed? What if…I can only imagine what if…joy, happiness, and excitement would not only bubble up, but would be uncontainable. Yes, out of the box, no longer boxed in.

What if…we lived today as if it were about to happen. What if…we called those things that are not as though they were, and really believed they could be. Yes, what if they changed suddenly today? What if… instead of being sad, down, depressed, we picked ourselves up by the bootstraps and said, "No more."

What if … regardless of what your spouse, child, friend, or boss said or didn't say, did or didn't do, we chose the high road? The road to victory, the road to success, the road to faith, the road to love? What if...sounds great, right?

How do we do the "What if?" How do we go from downcast to joy unspeakable while still in the same circumstance with no visual sign of change? The action starts with our heart that leads to the thoughts that then leads to the words, actions, and finally what we see unfolding in our lives. It just may not be in our time, our way but God is faithful.

Contributing Writer | Cinthia Shuster

## *Action, Application, Accountability*

Today, "What if..." we came together and agreed this really is the day that the Lord has made, and we really will be glad and rejoice in it? "What if..." we lived out what the Bible says and did those good works that always begin in our heart? Let's make a turnaround for the upturn in our lives. We affect and infect every person we are connected to with good or bad vibes. Therefore, choose life. Cast your cares upon the Lord, because He does care for you.

# PERSEVERANCE

*Let us throw off everything that hinders and the sin that
so easily entangles, and let us run with perseverance the
race marked out for us. Let us fix our eyes on Jesus, the
author and perfector of our faith. Hebrews 12:1-2*

Channing, Texas was home for the little dog named Baby Face and the mischievous little boy she loved. The boy's dad had died, and his mother worked long hours to provide for them. In fact, on this very day Baby Face, the boy and his mom were speeding down the highway on their way to a new home. They were headed to a town offering a more prosperous opportunity for the boy's mother.

Life can throw awful curves, as Baby Face discovered when an abrupt thunderous jolt propelled her into the front seat, into the middle of a confusing and scary place. Her young master and his mother were silent and bleeding. Men came. Desperately wanting to protect those she loved, Baby Face barked and growled to keep them at bay. One of the men grabbed her and threw her out of the car. Suddenly her only answer was to flee from the noise, confusion, and pain. Later, in search of the little boy, she returned to discover he was gone. And so, she began a journey of being reunited with the one she loved.

Day after day she searched; hungry, thirsty, and lonely. Playing over and over in her mind, "Press on and on and on." She knew if she remained steadfast in her search, she would eventually arrive in that place where her best friend would be waiting. At last she came upon a large building and, while circling it, caught the scent of the one she had so persistently sought. She waited patiently outside and, when the door finally opened, in she darted and ran without hesitation to the hospital room where the little boy lay. Baby Face bounded quickly onto his bed and rested her head quietly at his feet. Her pressing on was over, she was home, reunited with the young master she loved.

This little boy grew up and became a man. And undergirded by God's amazing Grace, in 1977 that man became my man, and we began a united journey of love, laughter, trials, and perseverance. He went home to rest at his Father's feet in 2010.

Contributing Writer | Carolyn Purdy

## *Action, Application, Accountability*

Sometimes life can be scary and confusing, and the only solution many find is to run and flee the world's unending pain and hurt. May the Lord help us, as His daughters, to come alongside lost and lonely people to offer them Jesus and encourage them to persevere in finding a Father at whose feet they may rest and heal.

# THE SPIRITUAL SAND DOLLAR

*For since the creation of the world God's invisible
qualities – his eternal power and divine nature – have
been clearly seen, being understood from what has been
made, so that men are without excuse. Romans 1:20*

ave you heard the legend of the sand dollar? Actually, it's
no legend at all. Its symbolism is based upon truth. If you
purchase a flat (not puffy) sand dollar that has been bleached
and hardened, you will be amazed at the spiritual types and shadows
imprinted both in and on the surface of this tiny little sea creature.

The Bible declares God's grace as being poured out for all who
believe, but only after Jesus' body was hung on the cross. It took Jesus'
fulfillment of the law and sacrifice to give us a grace like no other,
based on a new and better covenant. Grace is God's unmerited favor,
which is unearnable, but it is also a type of empowerment to withstand
challenging situations. And traditionally, five is the number of grace.

If you study the sand dollar, you will find the Poinsettia Christmas
flower on one side, representing Jesus' birth. On the other side you
will find the Easter Lily, representing His death and resurrection. The
Easter Lily also has a five-pointed star of Bethlehem in its center. Both
flowers have five petals, representing God's grace. In addition, the sand
dollar's frame has five holes. Four of them are in positions that appear
to be hands and feet (Jesus' endured the nails that formed holes in His

hands and feet). The fifth hole is centered at the bottom, representing the wound that Jesus' experienced from the sword that pierced his side.

Most Christians know that after His baptism, the Holy Spirit descended like a dove upon Jesus. God then declared, "This is my Son, whom I love, in Him I am well pleased." As stated before, in both the Old and New Testaments, grace could not be appropriated until a sacrifice was made, which included the breaking of the body (so to speak) through death, and the shedding of blood. In the New Testament, Jesus' body had to be broken by death before the Holy Spirit could be sent to dwell and lead us unto all truth.

So the *coup the grâce* is this: Only when you break the sand dollar's body in two, will you find five little doves that inhabit the creature's outer shell. Yes, five doves come tumbling out every time. By the way, the phrase I just used, *coup the grâce*, means *stroke of grace* in French. So these little doves represent the Holy Spirit, and five represents God's grace, poured out only through the breaking of Jesus' body on the cross. This beautiful sea urchin is full of symbolism that points to our Lord's work on the cross.

The sand dollar's given name came from its appearance on shore. Once the creature died and washed inland, the sun would bleach it white, and it would resemble a large silver coin, not unlike the old American and Spanish dollars. I personally believe the sand dollar's name is providential, as its figuration of Christ has eternal value.

Contributing Writer | Sheila Ninowski

## *Action, Application, Accountability*

Purchase a few sand dollars, and at every opportunity, share this symbolism with your friends and family to encourage their faith. God's creative footprint is everywhere.

# RECOGNIZING GOD'S DIRECTION

*Delight yourself in the Lord and he will give you
the desires of your heart. Psalm 37:4*

I prayed for God's direction for months. Should I travel to South Korea to attend an international board meeting? My flesh answered, "Stay home. It's a long flight, you don't speak the language, and you have pressing needs and priorities." I didn't want my selfish fears or desires to stand in the way of God's plan, but He had given no peace or firm direction.

I recalled how the twelve disciples huddled in a boat during a storm. They were so terrified they mistook Jesus for a ghost when He walked toward them on the water. Yet one disciple, Peter, boldly cried out in the midst of the wind and waves, "Lord, if it is you, command me to come to you on the water," and Jesus said, "Come." That day, Peter briefly walked on the water while the other eleven missed the opportunity. I preferred to be like Peter, stepping out in faith rather than missing what God had planned.

Through His word, He gently reminded me to delight myself in Him and He would give me the desires of my heart. I realized I was praying for God's direction, but my flesh had already decided I didn't want to go. I asked God to exchange my desires for His. I began seeking His priorities and asked for the motivation to serve and glorify Him rather than my flesh. Like Peter calling out to the Lord, I prayed, "Lord, if it is you calling me to South Korea, will you show me?"

And He did. He impressed on my heart that He was calling me, and He also confirmed in other ways. Things fell into place so the 'pressing needs' of home were covered. My dog sitter was available to care for my beloved pet. I got a flight with other board members traveling to the same location. God even provided airline mileage points to cover the cost of the airfare.

The final confirmation came when I attended a dinner event honoring the South Korean ministry where I served as a board member. Not only was I seated at the same table as the ministry President, but I was also touched by the faith stories shared by their speakers. Through a series of confirmations, the Lord provided clear direction. I was to travel to South Korea and attend the board meeting.

If you are seeking God's direction, remember this:

- God is faithful. He speaks to our hearts, through His Holy Spirit, His word, and His believers. He lines it all up to confirm His direction.
- God has eternal purposes and He invites us to join Him. Don't miss an opportunity because things appear difficult.
- God will exchange the desire of our heart to His desires if we seek Him and yield our will to His.
- God's timing, provision, and power are perfect.

Contributing Writer | Pat Gordon

## *Action, Application, Accountability*

Seek God's direction in all matters, large and small. If you're uncertain about whether He is the one calling, yet you want to obey

His will, then boldly ask, "Lord, if that's you calling me, show me." Then watch. He will answer and confirm the way you should go. Then obey. (He has called, equipped, and given each of us gifts to use, so be obedient and fulfill your calling.)

# There's Power in His Presence

*And I will ask the Father, and he will give you another*
*Counselor to be with you forever – the Spirit of truth.*
*The world cannot accept him, because it neither sees*
*him nor knows him. But you know him, for he lives*
*with you and will be in you. John 14:16-17*

One of the biggest keys to God's Kingdom is our authority and power. We are all destined to reign in this life, but many believers do not understand this. We have the same authority on this earth as when man was created. Jesus died to give back what Adam and Eve lost through disobedience.

It all starts with His presence, then moves to Holy Spirits revelations. Did you know that revelations of His nature are invitations to experience Him? Each time He reveals a piece of Himself, dwell there for a while. Learn more and ask questions. I have experienced many supernatural events, because the Holy Spirit is my teacher.

After giving the commission to 70 disciples, Jesus sent them in pairs to their hometowns, saying, "Go! I am sending you out like lambs among wolves. Do not take a purse or bag or sandals; and do not greet anyone on the road. When you enter a house, first say, Peace to this house. If someone who promotes peace is there, your peace will rest on them; if not, it will return to you." Luke 10:3-6

This is central in His instruction for our ministry. It is tied directly to our ability to recognize the Presence of the Holy Spirit. If we are not conscious of the impact only the Holy Spirit can make, whose power are we going in? When we reduce the power of God to principles that bring breakthrough, we cheapen the journey. People who desire principles above Presence seek a kingdom without a king.

God wants us to be vulnerable in our abandonment to His purposes. So, unless He shows up to provide and direct, it will not work. We can do nothing in our own strength, and we should do nothing for our own glory. All the glory belongs to the Lord. Let the manifest presence of God go with you on our assignment and He will make dangerous places become safe.

Contributing Writer | Liz Morris

## *Action, Application, Accountability*

Do you walk in vulnerable abandonment to the purposes and plans of God? Have you surrendered your pride so He can work through you? Surrender your will to His so He can truly work.

# LEARNING TO TRUST

*Trust in the Lord with all your heart, and do not lean on
your own understanding. In all your ways submit to Him
and He will make your paths straight. Proverbs 3:5-6*

I n one of my toughest seasons, I cried, "God, I don't trust You!" And
I didn't. I believed it was God's fault when my parents divorced,
when my 21-year-old-brother died from suicide, and when my 17-
year marriage ended in divorce. I believed God had let me down time
after time. As a matter of fact, everyone I knew had let me down, and I
didn't trust anyone.

In the Bible, trust is mentioned 134 times, yet my logic was, "God,
how in the world can I trust you?" It was a long and arduous road in
learning that man's decisions are made through their free will and not
by God's design or plan.

On that day, God heard me and made Himself known. I often tell
friends, as soon as I was honest about my lack of trust in God, my eyes
were opened to see His faithfulness. I opened my heart to trust Him in
tiny things, and He was there. I reached out to Him through the years,
in bigger ways, to see if and how He would answer. His response was
often more than I expected. Sometimes He showed me that His ways
and plans were better than what I wanted or expected. His faithfulness
strengthened my trust.

Along life's journey, God gave me a dream of using my pain for His purpose. The calling was to help women work through their pain, disappointments, and failures. Could I fully trust Him to birth this dream? Would He be my provider, sustainer, comforter, teacher, and companion as I walked through the five years of training? He proved His faithfulness as my fifty-year life journey brought me to my path of purpose. In hindsight, I see His orchestration in using everything from my past as a training ground to serve women, helping them overcome their pain.

A dear friend has often said, "When God shows up, He shows off." and He certainly has in my journey to trust Him.

Contributing Writer | Cindy Hyde

## *Action, Application, Accountability*

Pray: "Father, thank you for showing me so mercifully that I can trust you. Time and time again, you show up and show off. You deserve the glory for the many things you orchestrate in my life to bring beauty from ashes. Amen."

# A Road Trip to Remember

*On my bed I remember you; I think of you through the watches of the night. Because you are my help, I sing in the shadow of your wings. My soul clings to you; your right hand upholds me. Psalm 63:6-8*

We were three pictures away from Grandma's house. Three state lines to cross before reaching our traditional vacation destination. Three times for Dad to rouse us kids from car games or slumber against the station wagon window. "We're crossing another state line. Let's get our picture," he announced from the driver's seat. Our answer was a mix of yawns, snorts, and moans, "Do we have to?" "Yes, years from now we need to remember where we traveled," he replied, "C'mon!" We tumbled out of the car. Four kids, Mom, Dad, and our Chihuahua, El Toro.

Dad lined us up. We leaned against the sign posts and rolled our eyes as he took the next five minutes to adjust every aperture and setting on his new Canon camera. Then he realigned us under the "Welcome to ___." (You fill in the state, and we have the picture.)

Slides actually. Carefully dated and stacked in sequence in the scratched and dented metal box Dad purchased to store our memories. I flipped the two latches down, now stiff from years of neglect and disuse. I peeled back the duct tape Dad put on either side of the locks as extra insurance in case the chest fell off the top shelf in his closet.

Inside … our childhood memories. Every state line we crossed. Every Easter egg we hunted. I lingered over every house we moved into, Santa we visited, and Christmas gift we opened under our silver tinsel tree. In an afternoon, I watched, and remembered, how my family grew under Dad's watchful eye.

I mumbled a prayer of thanks to Dad and apologized for grousing at every stop to stand by a state welcome sign. I hoped he heard it from his front seat in heaven. I heard him say again, "We need to remember where we traveled, what we did."

Likewise, God encouraged His Israelite children to remember their road trip. As He led them through the desert, He often repeated one word, "Remember." Their road trip was a testimony to how much He loved them. Remember escaping slavery in Egypt to cross the Red Sea and Jordan on dry land. Remember victories over enemies and daily provision. Recognize and remember the great lengths their Father-God went to save and shape them no matter how many times they complained or turned their backs on Him. Remember and pass the stories on to future generations so that they, too, might seek and know His love.

Mom often said, "Your father loves and lives for you kids. He would do anything for you." And so is the love of our Father in heaven. Remember.

Contributing Writer | Gloria Ashby

## *Action, Application, Accountability*

Hindsight gives us 20/20 vision. What memories from the past allow you to see God's provision, direction, and love in a new way? Say a prayer of thanksgiving to God for His faithfulness.

# PRAISE YOU IN THE STORM

*But now I urge you to keep up your courage, because not one
of you will be lost; only the ship will be destroyed. Last night an
angel of the God whose I am and whom I serve stood beside
me and said, – Do not be afraid, Paul. You must stand trial
before Caesar; and God has graciously given you the lives of all
who sail with you; so keep up your courage, men, for I have faith
in God that it will happen just as he told me. Acts 27:22-25*

We all walk through storms, but every storm is an opportunity to grow in faith and love. God allows us to be in the storm to break apart the devil's work. In the storm, He perfects us. He allows us to change. The storm can bring us out of loneliness, unforgiveness, unhealthy dependencies, hopelessness, fear, and anger. It can also build our faith in God, if we let it. Did you know that one obedient life can invite the favor of God to many others in the storm?

We must weather the storm so our character is perfected by God's grace. When we learn to trust the Father for everything, placing our fears, doubts and discouragements at the foot of the cross, we are changed. As we allow Him to change our character and belief about who He is, we are on the road to victory. We then believe Him for provision, family, spouse, boss, health, loss, courage, culture, character and miracles. Our

166

belief grows easier and our faith produces miracles everywhere we go. The Holy Spirit then becomes our teacher in the place of man.

The apostle Paul believed God would protect him through all of life's storms, trials and tribulations. He believed so completely that when a poisonous viper bit him, he flung it off and kept working. On the other side of our perfect storm, we realize the serpent is all bite and no venom. We see the results of what Jesus died to give; a life where we know God whispers through the rain and we learn to praise Him in the storm.

If you are ever in a storm like Paul, do not be afraid. Keep your courage, have faith in God, and it will be done just as He told you it would. Take hold of your faith, and watch it produce those miracles everywhere you go, just like Paul. If you will praise him in your storms and allow him to change you into his likeness, storms will obey.

Contributing Writer | Liz Morris

## *Action, Application, Accountability*

One person obedient to God brings favor to everyone on the ship during a storm. Look at your lifestyle. Do you throw fits as you walk through a storm rather than walking in obedience, trusting God? Commit to be the one who brings favor to your group, your household, your entire city by walking in obedience to God.

# Right Job, Right Time

*For I know the plans I have for you, declares the Lord, plans to prosper you and not to harm you, plans to give you hope and a future. Jeremiah 29:11*

I knew long before anyone else that my job was not a good fit, but I was the sole breadwinner for the family. My daughter was a junior in high school and headed for college. This was not the best time to make another move. Couple that with the fact I was 60 years of age, which is not the easiest time to compete for a job.

I wasn't involved in a church; too busy working, of course. But I knew I had to prepare for the inevitable. In my gut, I knew I would not make it long term in this job, and I needed help. The first thing was to turn my focus back to the Lord. I pulled out my Bible and daily devotional, I prayed and planned. My husband and I found a church and started attending regularly.

Next steps were to get the house ready to sell, update my Linked-in profile, polish my resume, network, and journal my thoughts to reinforce the positives; i.e. my personal mission, best skills, goals, type of work I do well, environment I'd like to work in, etc. I had no idea where this would lead but I put my faith in the Lord and kept moving forward.

My gut was right. The job would not work out much longer. I took the initiative to develop a plan with my boss. I would move out of my current job and work on a special project for which I had unique skills. I would resign after my daughter's graduation. We sold our house, downsized and moved into a small apartment on a temporary basis, and readied ourselves for what was to come.

One day, out of the blue, I received a phone call from a recruiter. He told me the company (I'd never heard of) came across my Linked-in profile, and I was the perfect candidate for a job they were creating. Would I be willing to interview? After multiple interviews, I received a job offer which came two weeks prior to my last day in the former job. I never missed a paycheck. It was the perfect job and an excellent place to work prior to my ultimate retirement.

The learning was clear. Ask the Lord to help you, seek to find your unique, God-given gifts and talents, knock on doors to explore options, but always trust in the Lord that the right opportunity will come at the right time.

Contributing Writer | Rebecca Campbell

## *Action, Application, Accountability*

In scripture, God promises to be our guide and lead us to the path of purpose. When you come to a crossroads in life and have decisions and choices to make, lean into Him for wisdom. He speaks through scripture, others, and circumstances. Sometimes He speaks through promptings in our spirit. Lean into Him during your quiet time, Bible study time, and prayer time. His greatest desire is for you to know Him intimately. Knowing Him in this way gives you confidence of being aligned with His best life through every choice and crossroad of decision.

# STANDING ON THE PROMISES

*I am with you and will watch over you wherever you go, and
I will bring you back to this land. I will not leave you until
I have done what I have promised you. Genesis 28:15*

We all experience them at one time or other, broken promises. Some unfulfilled on purpose. Others, unintentionally. A few, we may still hold out hope to be kept. I remember times of grief and loneliness from broken relationships. But I also remember some forty years ago, standing at God's altar with the man who promised to have me, hold me, and love me. And he has, even when I fall short of the Proverbs 31 "wife of noble character."

After worrying about remaining childless, I remember standing by a baby crib, amazed the tiny bundle sleeping there was my newborn daughter. And then sixteen years later I worried about her safety as she backed out of the garage and onto the streets solo for the first time. Then I remember every night she opened the back door to let me know, "I'm home!"

I remember the car accident when I found myself on the pavement in the middle of five o'clock traffic wondering where my car went. And I remember later in the Emergency Room when the doctor pronounced that I escaped injury with nothing more than torn pantyhose and a ripped dress. I remember standing in disbelief when I didn't get the promotion I was certain was rightfully mine. Then, I remember later standing in my new employer's office, stunned yet thrilled with the "better-than-I-could-ever-imagine" opportunity that opened to me.

I remember standing at the foot of my father's bed when the doctor said he had a disabling heart condition but could live four to five years if he took care of himself. Then, I remember standing at the foot of his grave, but seventeen years later, and flooded by the precious time and memories God gifted me since his diagnosis.

Through every twist and turn in life, in each joy and sorrow, mountain or valley, I realized I was standing on promises. I still stand on them today. God's promise of His faithfulness. His promise to always be with me and for me, through it all. His promise to weave all things to my good if only I trust in Him.

In the words of R. Kelso Carter's beloved hymn, I am...

> *Standing on the promises that cannot fail, when the howling storms of doubt and fear assail, by the living Word of God I shall prevail, standing on the promises of God.*

For these promises I am eternally thankful.

Contributing Writer | Gloria Ashby

## *Action, Application, Accountability*

Psalm 40:2 says "He put my feet upon the rock and gave me a firm place to stand." God is faithful in ways we fail to see until we get our hindsight vision. As Gloria demonstrated in this devotional, God brings us through difficulty and storms in ways that increase our faith. What is your story of God's faithfulness? Remember it, write it, and share it with someone today.

# LUCKY PENNY?

*The prayer of a righteous man is powerful
and effective. James 5:16*

F ound a lucky penny lately? I haven't in quite a while. Many years
ago, when I stumbled across an abandoned one laying on the
sidewalk, the Holy Spirit counseled me to think of it as a "blessing"
penny. Since that day, when I find a coin, I pause and wait for the Spirit
to place someone on my heart that needs a special blessing, then I lift a
prayer for them. If it's a nickel or dime, I pray for the five or ten people
He brings to my heart. One day I found four quarters. Upon returning
home, I retrieved a piece of paper and listed 100 names, offering quick
bullet prayers for all.

I've also used "blessing" pennies as a witnessing gift, asking whoever
is with me if they know anyone who needs a special blessing. Given a
name and possibly a need, I lift a short prayer on their behalf. Once
home, I have a personal "treasure chest" for these coins. They remind me
of the eternal value of the prayers we offer for one another. In Revelation
5:8 we read, "they were holding golden bowls full of incense, which are
the prayers of the saints."

When finding a coin, there have been occasions when the Holy
Spirit nudged me to send a note to the person He placed on my heart.
I include the blessing penny, explaining they were who the Lord felt
needed a special blessing that day. Many times, I have been personally

blessed in finding one of these treasured coins, because I am the one in a crisis or distracted and caught up in the busyness of the world. I am grateful for these little reminders of the Lord's faithful presence in my life.

Contributing Writer | Carolyn Purdy

## Action, Application, Accountability

People will say that a penny doesn't buy much in our world today. But I know how wrong they are. Don't pass by that lonely coin laying in your path. Pick it up. It's a blessing waiting for someone God knows needs it. And perhaps that someone is you.

# RELEASE AND EMBRACE

*Cast all your anxiety on him because he cares for you. 1 Peter 5:7*

R elease is a liberating word. Every time I think or say it, I find myself exhaling a long, relaxed breath. And yet, release is one of the most difficult things to do. Why? What makes it so difficult to release the painful residue from our past? You'd think we'd gladly pitch our torment to the wind, but instead sometimes we adhere to it, unable to let it go. Eventually our arms become weary, as we cling with white knuckles to our distress. The problem is this: The pain will ultimately outweigh our capacity to hold onto it.

If we're ever going to embrace the joy that life has in reserve, we must first release what's weighing us down in the first place. And if our arms are loaded with affliction, they can never be extended to embrace the good. We must simply find a way, some way, to replace the negative with an appreciation of the beauty that's all around us. Our great Shepherd will lead us to the still waters, but only if we let Him. And through it all, we must learn to accept the love we receive from others, and most importantly, we must learn to love ourselves.

Open your arms wide extended to the Lord, take a deep breath, release, and embrace His goodness.

Contributing Writer | Stephanie McDaniel
Excerpt from her book, *Girl undone, Girl redeemed.*
*Living a legacy of life after trauma (Published 2020)*

## *Action, Application, Accountability*

Your character is not defined by your mountain top experiences; it is built by difficulties, hard times and failures. Learn and grow from your mistakes; that's what they are for. They are blatant keys to change you into His likeness; the One who created you from the foundation of the world.

When burdened or weighed down by any circumstance or situation in life, take a deep cleansing breath and try the following:

1. Write what burdens you on a sheet of paper or notecard.
2. Let God know you're giving it to Him, leaving it at His altar.
3. Then release it. Wad it up and throw it away or burn it in your fireplace.
4. Now, on a notecard, write how you are blessed today. Post it at your desk, dressing mirror or some other place and read it throughout the day. And, every time your thought turns to the released burden, focus on the blessing card.

# The Business of Life

*Commit to the Lord whatever you do, and
your plans will succeed. Proverbs 16:3*

My husband and I have been buying foreclosed homes, remodeling and reselling them for the last 25 years. My kids say we should have done a television program years ago, then we could have been the original Chip and Joanna. I don't know about that, but I do know having the right business partner means everything.

In life and in business the scriptures tell us to be wise, to do our homework, and to seek the counsel of experts. Ultimately, however, the best business decision anyone can make is to have the right business partner, which is the Lord Himself. We find ourselves in a wonderful position of blessing when we learn to submit all our choices and decisions to the Lord, including those in respect to work and finances.

There are many stories about houses we bought after prayer and a leading of the Holy Spirit, only to later discover they were a far better purchase than we realized. For instance, the house would be in a newly announced up-and-coming area, or across the street from a proposed park, or about to be rezoned to a better school district, or before a huge corporation announced they were relocating to the area and needed lots of housing.

Only the Lord knows what the future holds and what is around every corner. God is a loving Father who delights in blessing His children who are in a position for Him to show favor. God allows us to choose where we invite Him into our lives. If we don't invite Him and include Him, He lets us live without His guidance. But why would we, when we have access to the greatest all-knowing counselor ever?

Contributing Writer | Kathleen Watson

## *Action, Application, Accountability*

In Malachi 3:10, God says, "Test Me now in this … if I will not open for you the windows of heaven and pour out for you a blessing until it overflows." This is referring to the tithe, but it holds true with every aspect of our life. Yes, tithing will be one of the first directives God gives us as his business partners, but living on 90% of an income that is blessed by God is much better than living on 100% of an income which is not blessed by God. This is the only verse in the Bible where God says, Test Me. I challenge you today- ask God to be your business partner, submit your financial decisions to his leading, tithe 10% and watch every aspect of your life be abundantly blessed.

# Trust the Holy Spirit

*And without faith it is impossible to please God, because anyone who comes to him must believe that he exists and that he rewards those who earnestly seek him. Hebrews 11:6*

Though I knew of Christ and loved Him from an early age, I didn't ask Him into my life until I was fourteen years old. Even though I was basically what the world calls a "good girl", it was a radical transformation. Jesus filled a void I never knew was there and brought a peace I didn't know was missing. He also brought the most astounding love I had ever felt. We had an intimate relationship and talked daily. He gave me assurance that my eternity was secure. And He gave me confidence that there was a big God who cared enough that He spoke clearly to little ole' me on my day of salvation.

At sixteen, I heard about the baptism of the Holy Spirit at my boyfriend's church. Rather than seeking advice from my parents, the pastor, or others about this spiritual gift, I went directly to the Holy Spirit. The following Tuesday, I said to my boyfriend, "If this really is of the Lord, and I read in the Bible that it is, then I want it." We began to pray. Suddenly in my mind I heard words that were not English. I began to speak them out loud, over and over. It was different than anything I had heard before. But I knew it was from the Holy Spirit because there was such peace.

Three nights later, my boyfriend's church hosted a prophetic minister. We were both serious about the Lord, so we attended the event. The gentleman taught and then he started speaking prophetic words over people. I wanted to walk to the front of the church and have a prophetic word spoken over me, but I was scared. So, I went to the bathroom to pray. It was as though an angel sat on one shoulder and a demon on the other. One said, go . . . the other said don't. I returned to my seat and gathered the courage to walk to the front of the church. It was a life changing experience.

The prophetic minister laid his hands on my shoulders and spoke these words: "My daughter, my daughter, I gave you the gift of tongues three days ago." What? How did he know? No one knew except me and my boyfriend. He continued, "I have all my gifts for you, in fact I have a ministry for you far greater than your mind could ever imagine." The gentleman then said to me, "Is this true?" I answered, "Yes sir." He continued, "Well the Lord said He has all His gifts for you, so just pray your prayer language out loud and let's ask the Holy Spirit for the gift of interpretation." I said, "okay" and began speaking my prayer language out loud. Then I heard the same voice from my salvation experience give me the interpretation in English. I spoke it out loud. Now remember, I had never seen anyone do this before. But I knew the Lord was working in me, I knew there was so much more than what I had been taught in church, and I wanted it. And now I knew that one day I would have a ministry far greater than my mind could imagine. That prophetic word is now coming to pass after 44 years of waiting.

Contributing Writer | Liz Morris


## *Action, Application, Accountability*

If God promised you something or spoke to you prophetically, do not faint while you wait. His timing and season are perfect. As you wait, study the covenant God established with those who walk in obedience to Him. You can only operate in faith according to the knowledge of His will and desire for your life. You must have a clear photograph of the will of God so your faith can implement it. Diligently seek the things that God has in store for you and acknowledge the things He has already done for you. Begin today to start moving your mountains. It will be well worth the wait.

# ATTAINING THE MIND OF CHRIST

*As a man thinketh, so is he. Proverbs 23:7 KJV*

D r. Caroline Leaf's book *Who Switched off my Brain²* stated, "Research shows that as much as 87% to 95% of mental and physical illnesses are a direct result of toxic thinking – proof that our thoughts affect us physically and emotionally".

Observing family members and friends for the last thirty to forty-five years, I watched them make choices that intentionally and unintentionally deflected them from God and caused them to adopt rebellious or cynical attitudes. In some cases, they literally thought themselves into oblivion. Thoughts lead to behavior, and behavior leads to habits. Therefore, it is vital we guard our thought life with vigilance.

As a result of tainted thinking, some of those family members became alcoholics, losing jobs and homes, or developing diseases. They gradually became dysfunctional and inappropriately dependent upon others, unaware of the dark transformation that took place over time. In many ways, their mindlessness has sabotaged their destiny, not to mention the pain it generated in the people around them. Mindless is the key word here, which is the opposite of mindful – that is, being fully aware and thoughtful of one's emotions, their root source, and their effects upon self and others.

I am convinced that Caroline Leaf's theory is correct. I realize there are chemical imbalances that can affect one's mental stability, but people can make cognitive and behavioral choices that lead them down the path of destruction. Unfortunately, that path is often a slow and deceptive one not realized until it is too late. If I knew at a young age what I know now, perhaps I could have warned them. If they knew at a young age how their attitude would eventually affect them, maybe they would have made an adjustment. What we choose to think upon affects us.

It doesn't matter whether circumstances (out of our control) taints us, or we corrupt ourselves. Either way, we can become cynical and suspicious of everything and everyone around us if we are not careful to guard our hearts against such presumption. The Bible tells us to "Do to others as you would have them do to you" (Mark 6:31). That also means believing and seeking the best in others. Isn't that what we want for ourselves?

Contributing Writer | Sheila Ninowski

## *Action, Application, Accountability*

To cultivate the mind of Christ, we can do several things: Renew our minds daily in God's word. Spend time in intimate worship of the Lord, which is spirit to spirit, and allows room for more truth to be revealed. Give thanks for all things, as thanksgiving has a cleansing, sanctifying effect on everything around us. Think positively and cast down any vain imaginings that cause us to ruminate on the negative. Think on whatever is true, honorable, right, pure, lovely, worthy of praise, or of a good report. Believe the best in others (which, by the way, is how God sees us). Finally, pray in the spirit. If you speak in tongues, utilize your prayer language often. As such, you are praying God's will into your life, and affecting the spirit realm. If we practice these things in the good times, we will be fortified to handle the hard times.

# WHAT DO YOU WANT
# ME TO DO FOR YOU?

*Go, said Jesus, your faith has healed you.*
*Immediately he received his sight and followed*
*Jesus along the road. Mark 10:51*

I vividly remember the encounter. The Lord's presence filled my room. It felt as if every moving molecule had been vacuumed out and a perfect stillness and reverence had entered. I became motionless and in awe. From the center of the room, I heard the Lord's voice, "What do you want Me to do for you?" I was stunned. I had fasted and prayed, beseeching the Lord for restoration, yet I had doubts He heard my cry and would answer. Overwhelmed, I instinctively knew whatever I voiced would be done. I measured my thoughts. No words came from my lips.

As days went by, the question replayed, "What do you want Me to do for you?" The Lord visited me, in answer to my cry; yet, I was unable to voice the deepest intentions of my heart. Why was I unable to articulate what I wanted? Why was it so hard to embrace that He wanted to respond?

Many of us are doubtful the Lord hears our cry, or better yet, that He would ask, "What do you want Me to do for you?" Yet, the gospel of Mark reminds us this query is from the heart of God. Remember blind Bartimaeus who sat by the road begging? When he heard that Jesus was passing by, he cried out to Him. Jesus knew the deepest desire of Bartimaeus' heart; yet, He inquired, "What do you want Me to do for you?" "Rabboni" he answered, "that I may receive sight." Jesus responded, "Go your way; your faith has made you well." And immediately he received his sight (Mark 10:46-51).

Two more times, the Lord returned to me posing the same question. On the third occasion, I was ready to articulate the deepest desire of my heart, a desire He already knew, yet a desire He wanted me to know. "I want you to put my life in order."

I wish I could tell you that, like blind Bartimaeus, my life immediately changed. Although the Lord answered my request for restoration, it took many years before I experienced the fullness of His answer. The Lord had to come to me on three occasions to invoke a heart response, as He knew my heart was clouded with doubts, unable to respond to Him on the first or second occasion.

From this encounter, I am reminded how the Apostle Peter denied the Lord in Jerusalem, and how the Lord came to him as the glorified and resurrected Christ, to bring restoration and to obtain a heart response. "Simon son of Jonah, do you love me more than these?", the Lord asked Peter. "Simon, son of Jonah, do you love Me?", the Lord asked Peter a second time. "Simon, son of Jonah, do you love Me?", the Lord inquired a final time (John 21:15-17). These three inquiries were not without significance. They were purposeful and intentional, meant to restore the Apostle and to eliminate any doubt, guilt and condemnation from the three times Peter had denied the Lord (John 18:13-27). Restoration is the heart of our Lord and Savior.

Contributing Writer | Christina L. McCracken, J.D.
Taken from her book, *Divine Restoration,*
*From Counselor to counselor*

## *Action, Application, Accountability*

The Lord comes to us today and asks, "What do you want Me to do for you?" Whether you respond on the first, second or third inquiry, respond. He poses this question to restore us, our heart, our faith, our relationship with Him, and to destroy any doubt, guilt and condemnation in our heart. If He were to come to you today with this question, would you be able to respond? If not, ask Him to reveal any doubt, guilt or condemnation that may be clouding your heart and veiling your trust and faith in Christ.

# WHATEVER LIFE BRINGS

*Hear my prayer, Lord, and listen to my cry; come
to my aid when I weep. Psalm 39:12*

This journey called life ... is filled with laughter and tears,
blessings and fears. In all these moments, God whispers special
treasures for us to discover.

This hit home when I learned a dear friend had stage four cancer
and only a few months to live. I cried for two weeks, asking, "God, what
is this? Why can't I stop crying?" The Holy Spirit whispered, "This is
an old fear that life will take away your joy and happiness." God gave
me peace to trust Him for my future while also grieving for my friend
and his family. He assured me that whatever life brings, He and I will
journey through it together.

Contributing Writer | Vanda Tougas

## Action, Application, Accountability

When have you cried tears you could not understand? Did you
ignore them or tap into them with prayer? Are you crying now? Ask
God what He wants to reveal to you, then listen deeply. He will show
you the path to peace.

# IT'S TIME TO CELEBRATE

*But the father said to his servants, 'Quick! Bring the best robe and put it on him. Put a ring on his finger and sandals on his feet. Bring the fattened calf and kill it. Let's have a feast and celebrate. For this son of mine was dead and is alive again; he was lost and is found.' So they began to celebrate. Luke 15:22-24*

Before a wedding, there is a shower, a pre-wedding celebration to prepare the bride. For the groom, there is a bachelor party, a pre-wedding celebration to celebrate his last days of being single. When we graduate from school, college, have a birthday, anniversary or any other special day, it is normal and expected to celebrate. To somehow recognize the day or event and have a "pause moment" of joyful review, expectation and hope of what is to come or review what we are commemorating. Why do we do this? Why do we set aside a time to celebrate? It is to remember the past, the hallmarks of our life and go forward. It is also to stir our faith, hope, and expectancy for the future, in the case of a baby or wedding shower.

What if every day we lived from this same place of "time to celebrate" with a positive knowing that God has good dreams, desires, and expectancies of our heart, although we may not see them right now, yet we know they are being prepared for us? How do we know? Because He says so. What if we chose to purposely celebrate the good things every day rather than focus and dwell on the bad ones?

What if we turned our attitude and renewed our mind to what God has to say in the Holy Scripture? How do we do this? How can we renew our mind? Whatever we feed our eyes, ears, heart, and mind will be the outcome of what comes out of our mouth. Words are containers for life or death. Choose wisely, choose life. How do we know the difference? It is as simple as saying the word or words. Everything has a value or "vibe"; we often hear the word "energy."

It is easy to dismiss or laugh at this culture based on familiar spirits and gods not related to the True and Living God. We are not to laugh, ridicule or make fun of others. Rather, we are to share the good news of what our experience is with Truth. We must celebrate the victories, miracles, and continual turnarounds we have, even if not at this moment, but those that have unfolded throughout our lifetime. Others will ask what our "it factor" is and then we can share the good news of Jesus.

Contributing Writer | Cinthia Shuster

## *Action, Application, Accountability*

Today, start a celebration journal. Think on and record things from your day that are true, honorable, lovely, of a good report, filled with virtue and love. Celebrate on the high things, and you will find the low things begin to get much lower and finally have no tone or tune in your life. This renews your mind in the things of God, the good and eternal things that will last. These things also have the power to produce different outcomes for your "here and now." We are eternally built to last and God has made a way for us to accept that eternal life pass. That Way is Jesus. Today, if you know Him as your Lord and King, it's time to celebrate and share this good news with others.

# HOW SATAN USES PRIDE AGAINST YOU

*Pride goes before destruction, and a haughty spirit before a fall. Proverbs 16:18*

The devil knows if he can get us into pride, we will eventually fall. The Lord warns us many times against pride, but the world tempts us tremendously. The scary part is we don't even recognize it.

Do you judge others by their appearance? Do you criticize people on television? Do you want others to see you driving your expensive car? Do you try to be the center of attention? Do you talk about how much money you have or spend?

Do you judge someone by their education, weight, manner of speech? Or by their tattoos, piercings and colored hair? Maybe it's by the color of their skin or ethnicity? Do you post your extravagant possessions or travels on social media for others to see? Do you judge church denominations or the way a pastor delivers a message?

The minute we have a negative opinion of anyone, whether in thought or word, it is pride. We all have it. Pride is Satan's number one tool. This is how he separates us, so we won't be effective in God's Kingdom.

Contributing Writer | Liz Morris

## *Action, Application, Accountability*

Satan has many schemes to turn you from God. To battle this scheme, pray: "Lord, show me the areas of pride in my life so I can lay them at the altar. Help me look for the positive in people and situations rather than judging them. Amen."

# WHEN TROUBLE STRIKES

*The Lord himself goes before you and will be with you;*
*he will never leave you nor forsake you. Do not be*
*afraid; do not be discouraged. Deuteronomy 31:8*

I was sitting in the dentist chair when the receptionist brought in an urgent message to call my husband. His brief words, "I need you to come get me and take me to the Emergency Room. I need to have open heart surgery tomorrow." That's it. No explanations. He had gone for a routine test; no warning of any prior heart problems. The drive to get him was long and frightening, with fears and questions bubbling up. I called a friend and we prayed together.

That night in the Emergency Room, the on-site cardiologist told us he had initiated a referral to a Cardiac Surgeon. There was no time to research options or ensure we had the best surgeon. We were taking "pot-luck."

And yet, the most amazing thing happened. We Googled the referred surgeon and discovered his prior patients rated him 4.9 out of 5.0. He is considered one of the top heart surgeons in the state and is widely known as a Christian who prays with his patients prior to surgery. Add the fact that both of our children happened to be off work/out of school the day of the surgery, our pastor and wife were able to be there, and many friends and relatives came to the hospital to sit with us during the all-day delicate reconstructive surgery. It was a reminder God was not only with us, but ahead of the event, preparing the details that would ensure we were surrounded by love and had the best outcome possible from a near fatal circumstance.

Our lifestyle would forever be changed from that surgery, yet our trust in God was significantly strengthened. A reminder that no matter what trouble we face, He is already there.

Contributing Writer | Rebecca Campbell

## *Action, Application, Accountability*

What's at work here? Divine Providence or coincidence? Find the definition of Providence. God is always working behind the scenes to bring about His purposes for the nations and for individuals. Read the story of Joseph (Genesis 50:7-26) or read the book of Esther. Where have you seen God at work in human history? In your own life? Remember it; write it down. The next time you face trouble, remember He's already there.

# WORDS FOR THE HEART

*These commandments that I give you today are
to be upon your hearts. Deuteronomy 6:6*

D o you have a special life verse from scripture? In 1984, in a
small hospital chapel downstairs from where my husband
battled to save his transplanted kidney from rejection, I
surrendered my "I can if only..." to "I can't, but Jesus can." He whispered
into my heart, "You're going to be okay" and became not just Savior but
Lord of my life. Engraved on the tiny altar at the front of the chapel was
John 16:33, "In this world you will have trouble. But take heart! I have
overcome the world." Since that day, I have claimed this passage as my
personal life verse.

Years later in 2001, my daddy was hospitalized with a terminal
illness. I became my mother's caretaker during this difficult time as
she was already dealing with the early stages of Alzheimer's Disease.
Concern for her, grief, anxiety, and sibling stress continually tugged at
my awareness of the Lord's presence.

One evening, after returning to my parents' home from a particularly
tense day at the hospital, my mother and I suddenly saw a bright flash
of light and heard a booming thunderclap. Surprised because of the
sunshine we had experienced on our journey home, I peered out the
breakfast room window. Small hailstones began to fall all around the
house even though sunshine remained visible over the backyard stone

fence. After a few minutes, the pelting ceased, and I stepped outside to get a better view of the mysterious cloud that had delivered this surprise hail shower.

Looking up, I saw a beautiful vivid rainbow. Immediately I knew – God used His creation to gift me with a visual illustration of my life verse and the hope it promised at this difficult time. For in the midst of the sunshine of life, a storm of tribulation had arrived. But my heart could remain at peace because my God's promise of presence, comfort, and salvation remained true for me, my family and all who know Him.

Contributing Writer | Carolyn Purdy

## *Action, Application, Accountability*

What scripture verse speaks to your heart? Claim it, memorize it, and be alert to the Lord weaving it into the tapestry of your life. You might discover it as only the beginning of the heart verses He has woven throughout His Word especially for you.

# THE VINE | THE JOY OF THE LORD

*These things I have spoken to you that My joy may remain in you, and that your joy may be full. John 15:11*

I confess, there are times I don't feel the joy of the Lord. Many believers struggle with finding the joy that *remains in us*, as John 15:11 says, and we struggle with finding the fullness of joy.

As I recently contemplated the concept of "joy", I read the above scripture, but more importantly, I read the preceding passages. Prior to telling us that His joy can remain in us and that it can be full, Jesus tells us that He is the vine and we are the branches (John 15:5, 9). He instructs us to abide in His love, and then He promises us the fullness of joy. The two are directly connected.

As believers, if we aren't experiencing joy, it isn't a reflection of our salvation, but it is a reflection of how connected we are to the vine. A branch is still a branch when it is cut from the vine, but it quickly withers without the life-giving connection to the vine. If we aren't experiencing the fullness of joy, we need to check our connection to the vine, Jesus.

Contributing Writer | Elaine Sommerville

## *Action, Application, Accountability*

Is your connection with Jesus strong, or do you need to reconnect? When you can't tap into the joy of Jesus, maybe it is because you need to tap more into Jesus.

# WHAT ARE YOU DRAGGING?

*Do your best to present yourself to God as one approved,
a workman who does not need to be ashamed and who
correctly handles the word of truth. 2 Timothy 2:15*

I have something important to share. Listen carefully so you understand how something this simple, yet profound, can keep you bound and miserable for years. Are you ready?

*Be careful of dragging yesterday into today.*

Be careful of conjuring up negative feelings about past hurts, rejections, or pain in your life. Instead, learn to direct those emotions toward God's future for you. Your divine destiny is never predicated on your past abuses, failures, mistakes or sins. The Bible clearly says in all the gifts and callings God placed on your life, even if you don't know what they are, are *irrevocable*. Learn from your past mistakes and hurts and move on. Stop picking them up, stop being offended, and stop picking up other people's offenses. Stop dragging yesterday into today.

I see many people speaking negative things that typically come to pass. Remember, Satan hears your words, which are all he has to work with. Don't say, "Every year I get sick at such and such a time" or "I will never have enough money to have this or that". When you speak these things, you invite them to become reality.

Find scripture that pertains to Gods promises about you and quote them on a regular basis. You will have what you speak, whether good or bad. Some of God's promises are automatic and some must be coupled with your faith. If you don't know the difference, seek wisdom from the Holy Spirit and mature believers. The Bible says you must study to show yourself approved.

Many Christians live for the here and now and never contemplate their eternity. The everlasting part of their lives is forever.

Contributing Writer | Liz Morris

## *Action, Application, Accountability*

Read your Bible and find the promises that are rightfully yours. Then speak them until you believe them. When you do, your life will change forever.

# Working Through the Layers

*Now to him who is able to do immeasurably more than all we ask or imagine, according to His power that is at work within us. Ephesians 3:20*

This journey called life … is full of twists and turns, but if we are open to all life brings, God takes us to a better place than we can imagine.

I found the most freeing part of my relationship with God is to continually ask, "Lord, what is in me that keeps me from being who you fully made me to be? What do I still need to surrender?"

I listen for His answer and go deep within to find and heal the pain. Each layer worked through breaks open more pain, hurts and failures from the past. As those wounds are healed, God replaces them with joy, love and beauty. Healing takes a willing spirit and a strong faith.

Through God's guidance, I surrendered the pain of my childhood and forgave my parents for their mistakes, and God gave me freedom. I surrendered the hurt and betrayal of my marriage, and God showed me mercy, love, and a hope for the future. I surrendered my family to Him, and He showed me how to love with *His* love. I surrendered my dreams to Him, and He gave me a life I never imagined.

Contributing Writer | Vanda Tougas

199

## *Action, Application, Accountability*

Emotional and spiritual healing go hand in hand. It's hard work, but so worth it once you work through the layers of pain, wounds, and brokenness. Allow God to break you open, heal your pain, and fill you with Him. You will never be more of the you He created you to be.

# I'll Have What She's Having

*Thus, by their fruit you will recognize them. Matthew 7:20*

Have you ever gone into a restaurant and, as the hostess was leading you to a table, you scanned plates of food as you passed by? I tend to do this at new restaurants so I can get an idea of what the restaurant has to offer. Often food choices of others look so good that I want to try it myself. When the waiter asks, "May I take your order?" my response is, "Oh, I'll have what she's having, please."

We do the same thing with people we encounter. We watch behaviors, attitudes, motives, and lifestyles and are drawn to those people we want to emulate. This is not a bad thing. In 1 Corinthians 11:1, Paul told the Corinthians to follow his example. Why? Because they were new believers and didn't know much about the life and ministry of Christ. Paul told them to follow him because he followed Jesus. The best way to point new Christians to Christ is to point them to a Christian they can trust to walk in the ways of Christ.

We are exposed to many people throughout life. I find it interesting and intriguing that God made each of us completely different. We each have opinions, tastes, motives, desires. The list goes on. As we walk life's journey, we are called to be the very best God created us to be.

When faced with daily decisions and confrontations we should always consider the One who already knows everything and holds it all in His hands. Walking in this knowledge can sometimes be difficult because we are human. However, just as Paul was to the Corinthians, we are living examples of the One who lives inside of us. God's presence in us should be so obvious to the people we encounter that they desire Him too. And perhaps their hearts will be stirred with the same desire as my restaurant order, "Oh, I'll have what she's having, please."

Contributing Writer | Jackie Kenney

## *Action, Application, Accountability*

Pray: "Father, every day as I interact with others, please let them see You in me. Help me to always be the example You created me to be. Amen."

# THE VIOLENT TAKE IT BY FORCE

*And from the days of John the Baptist until now
the kingdom of heaven suffereth violence and the
violent take it by force. Matthew 11:12 KJV*

Have you ever wondered if bad things only happen to you? Why multiple 'not so good things,' seem to hit at one time? Perhaps in cycles? Do you doubt the very thing or person you once believed in, including yourself? Why and what has changed your mind, weakened your faith and resolve?

There are times in life when everything seems to soar along wonderfully. And have you noticed how your attitude and joy rise as well? Could it be that attitude and foundation determines our altitude?

Far too often we blame everything or anyone when life goes awry. What we need to do is step back and take a somber look (not condemning or depressing) at ourselves. Are we taking full responsibility to respond to the challenges, changes, and seeming difficulties that could actually be opportunities? The same passion that fueled the soaring things, can also be applied to the ones that are driving us down.

Today if you feel low, find someone to do something nice for—pay it forward with kindness, love, and caring. Be violent (pro-active) in your passion and action to get out of the low place, the valley, the bad attitude. Resolve to soar to a new one. Being "violent," isn't about having a tantrum and/or a rage episode. It speaks of a passion and persistent move toward the prize, like an Olympic athlete. Absolutely nothing stops them from reaching the finish line. How much more this persistence is relevant for us and our lives.

Contributing Writer | Cinthia Shuster

## *Action, Application, Accountability*

Where have you been limp in action, thought, or obedience? Be honest, then be on target. Set daily, weekly, monthly, and annual goals. Find an accountability partner that you can trust and take responsibility for new levels of achievement in your life. It begins with this—believing based on the Word of God, not how you feel, your past performance, or even the limitations of what you think you can do. You can do all things through Christ which strengthens you. Who knows, today could be the best day of your life.

# A WORK IN PROGRESS

*Being confident of this, that he who began a good*
*work in you will carry it on to completion until*
*the day of Christ Jesus. Philippians 1:6*

My two oldest grandsons, Jacob and Joseph, are young men now. When they were little guys, we would bring them to our home for a two-week summer vacation. Bedtime included story time. One of my favorite night reads was *Hermie, the Caterpillar* by Max Lucado.[3]

In the story, Hermie is envious of the other creatures he meets, because he feels he doesn't measure up to their beauty and/or talent. Each night in his prayer time, God assures him, "Don't worry, Hermie, I'm not through with you yet." Every time I read that line to the boys, I added, "Jacob, God's not through with you yet. Joseph, God's not through with you yet." After several repeats of this, Jacob looked straight at me and said, "CeCe, God's not through with you yet either." So, I was aptly reminded by my young grandson, I, also, was a worm.

All these years later, I remain sort of wormy, tempted to evaluate my worth by what the world deems beautiful, desirous, and successful. How thankful I am to have my Father; the Father who scripture assures does not focus on the things people in the world value as important. For, "people look at the outward appearance, but the Lord looks at the heart." 1 Samuel 16:7

Are you a little wormy like me? If your answer is yes, how about we put on God vision glasses as we observe and interact with one another and the world? We are a work in progress, and it is the Holy Spirit's counseling, teaching, and training in our hearts where the progress is being made.

Let's keep in mind the words of my little theologian grandson, God's not through with you yet. And until that time comes, let our praise be, "Now to Him who is able to do immeasurably more than all we ask or imagine, according to His power that is at work within us, to Him be glory, for ever and ever!" Ephesians 3:20-21

Contributing Writer | Carolyn Purdy

## *Action, Application, Accountability*

Father, thank you for Your Word that teaches, rebukes, corrects, and trains us as we await the time when Your work in and through us is complete. Give us patience and grace for ourselves and others as You walk us through this process of being made new in You. Amen.

# THE DALLAS DREAM TEAM
## WOMEN OF FAITH

*Before they call, I will answer; while they are*
*yet speaking, I will hear. Isaiah 65:24*

I f you are looking to transform your city, gather your girlfriends and
pray. I never dreamed one of the biggest benefits of starting *The
Dallas Dream Team* would be the placement of new and promising
friendships. I have met some of the most incredible ladies who love God
and enjoy giving unto "the least of these."

Look for givers, for there the Lord is. You will know them by their
fruit. Giving and serving are two of the greatest qualities of friendship.
That is my heart and I surround myself with people of like hearts. Stay
away from the stingy and self-serving, for they will not manifest God's
glory, they keep it for themselves.

When God released the mysterious sound at Pentecost at nine o'clock
in the morning, thousands of people gathered with the 120 already in
the upper room. No one really knows why the crowd gathered, but the
sound penetrated their hearts as it filled the air. It is as though God was
summoning His people. Imagine an atmospheric shift over an entire
city. On Pentecost things suddenly progressed from the anointing over
one man, Jesus, to the 120, and then to the 3,000 believers.

I believe *The Dallas Dream Team* will gather to an indistinguishable sound that reaches deep into the heart of every woman involved. I believe the unity we have will create a mighty move of God's spirit. I believe this is going to happen with us. It can also happen to you and your friends.

The potential of our movement is unlimited. As we continue to host Him and create a giving spirit towards every non-profit we encounter, God will power-charge the atmosphere of Heaven to rest on our movement, which will, in turn, force an atmospheric shift over our homes, businesses and city. I believe every woman involved has a heart for the hurting, helpless and homeless, and a desire to see God move.

This baptism of fire is for everyone. May this devotional inspire you to desire God's presence. Your spiritual journey is not about what you can accomplish for God; it's about the journey and those who walk with you, partaking of God more and more. Together we are better and stronger. As we cry out for a greater measure of God's presence and continue to give to those in need, He will use us for great and mighty exploits. As we contend for a greater measure of Him, He transforms us into His likeness. As we prioritize those things on God's heart, we learn to host Him well and release His glory on this earth and in our city.

May we all become the ultimate prototype in prayer to affect our city. May we do great exploits with signs and wonders so this generation will come to understand the fullness of the Holy Spirit's presence. We need to catch the fish and allow God to do the cleaning.

Ladies of *The Dallas Dream Team*, I love you dearly and believe in you. May our hearts and minds stay united and may we build His kingdom together. May we write many more devotionals about the things God is doing so we can change the lives of those who come after us. After all, every voice matters and everyone has a story to share.

Listed below are the founding members and partners who believed in the vision to help start this movement: Valerie, Sheila, Pat, Elizabeth, Gloria, Betty, Sue, Rebecca, Rosemary, Yvonne, Wendy, Leigh, Eliza,

Chris, Brenda, Helen, Alma Doll, Angel, Richi, Barbara, Carolyn, Christina, Cindy, Deb, Diane, Elaine, Jackie, Jan, Judy, Karen, Kathy, Kelli, Linda, Lisa, Lori, Lynnette, Mandy, Maria, Tencia, Marietta, Marva, Mary, Melanie, Paulette, Peaches, Reesa, Robin, Shari, Sheree, Sheri, Stacy, Terri, Tina, Vanda, Anne, Allison, April, Cheryl, Cory, Dianne, Jeanette, Joann, Joyce, Kathy, Katie, LisaKaye, Lyn, Rose, Wanda, Cinthia, Diane, Donna, Whitney, Shalonda.

Ladies, you are where God wants you. Every experience is part of His divine plan. Remember, we serve a God that can do far beyond what we can ask or imagine. God is working on your prayers.

Contributing Writer | Liz Morris

## *Action, Application, Accountability*

Here is your takeaway from this book of devotionals: Don't ever limit God to your present understanding of how He moves. What you know can keep you from what you need to know if you don't remain an apprentice. If you think you are an expert, you have chosen where you level off in your maturity. God still requires that key advancements in the Kingdom be made through childlikeness. So, sit back, relax and get ready to, 'Watch Him Move.'

# REFLECTIONS FOR TOMORROW

*Peter began to speak: I now realize how true it is that God does not show favoritism but accepts men from every nation who fear him and do what is right. Acts 10:34-35*

Father, I remind myself of who You are and Your attributes of power, might, provision, compassion, trustworthiness, and magnificence. You are Lord of All and King of Kings. There is none like You. You alone are fully faithful. I recall the specific times in life when You supernaturally heard my cry.

Abba, thank you for the privilege of praying for myself and my loved ones. Help us to see what is before us, not as challenges that overwhelm or burden us, but as opportunities to trust You more and rely on You to breathe wisdom and practical strategies to us. Thank You for Your provision today, knowing You are also aware of our needs for tomorrow.

Lord, we stir up within ourselves a grateful heart as You orchestrate much needed favor to go before us, as you have heard our prayers. We love that You provide so thoroughly for us that when we were separated from You and did not deserve it, You paid the cost for us. You are not withholding any good thing from us, and we are humble in our worship and praise of you. In Jesus Name. Amen.

Contributing Writer | Marva Hanks

# MY BEAUTIFUL SOUTHERN
# YA YA FRIENDSHIPS

*His master said to him, 'Well done, good and faithful slave. You were faithful with a few things; I will put you in charge of many things; enter into the joy of your master.' Matthew 25:21*

I grew up in the small town of Pine Bluff, Arkansas. The people were incredible, and the small hometown atmosphere was all I knew. I loved Dr. Pepper, ham and cheese sandwiches from Burger Chef, ice cream and cheerleading, and I spent a lot of time hanging out with girlfriends.

I had several close friends. Twelve of us still get together yearly even though we live all over the United States. We call ourselves the YA YA's.

YA YA number one is Debra; my BFF from birth. She is the most mature of us all and keeps us in line. She is the hostess with the mostest. Our mothers were close friends and we were born a month apart. Debra lives in Dallas, so I am blessed. She was the first person I told that I was getting married and she will always hold a special place in my heart.

Next is Denise; the hometown beauty queen, chosen by John Wayne. She resides in La Grange, Georgia. She is one of the sweetest people I know. I wish we lived closer. Her two daughters are gorgeous as well. In fact, one is a model (Malone) and was in Luke Bryan's music video, *Strip it Down* with her adorable model husband. Check it out.

Next, we have Sandy; the smartest one, who lives in Little Rock, Arkansas and loves to travel the world by herself. She never seems stressed even though she is an attorney. She never forgets any of our birthdays. She had her first grandchild recently and is truly smitten.

Jeanene married her high school sweetheart. She remembers every adventure, good and bad, and can tell a story like nobody's business. She lives in Peach Tree City, Georgia and is a great golf cart driver! We have made many of our adult memories in her condo in Panama City Beach. Thanks for all the great memories Jeanene!

Cindy was a little reserved while young but definitely came out of her shell. You would never know she birthed four boys because she is in great shape. She jogs daily and has beautiful naturally blonde hair. Cindy and I got stuck in an elevator one time and while she remained calm, I almost freaked out. I was calling on Jesus! I still don't like elevators. Cindy lives in Searcy, Arkansas and is married to a doctor.

Then there is Meredith. Next to Debra, I've known Meredith the longest because we grew up across the street from one another between first and sixth grades. In those years, we had dances in the carport and sang to Harper Valley PTA with our hairbrush microphones. She is a breast cancer survivor and one of the most positive and tenacious people I know.

Michelle is the tallest and by far the funniest of us all. She keeps us in stitches with her funny stories, like Jeanene, and is always ready to dance. She is our fashion model and dresses really hip. She works in media and always knows the latest scoop. She lives in Fayetteville; Arkansas and binges on Dave Matthews.

Then we have Carol who lives in Allen, TX. She married her high school sweetheart and they have three beautiful daughters. She is an excellent elementary school teacher, and I think she is the only one of us with both parents alive. Carol is loads of fun and we spent many a slumber party at her home. She and Lance love to grill out and float in their pool. Her first grandbaby arrived this year.

Next is Jill, whose dad was our high school principle. She lives in Atlanta, Georgia and loves to talk to me about the Lord. She and I are the early risers of the group and love to sit and have conversations and coffee on the balcony of Jeanene's condo on the beach. Jill has the most grandchildren of us all, so far.

Jeanne lives in Doylestown, Pennsylvania. We loved having slumber parties at her house as well because we could sneak out and roll people houses. Shhhh . . . I don't think that's legal, so don't do it. Jeanne is very caring and loving and always makes you feel special.

And last, but certainly NOT least, there's Nancy who graduated high school early and moved to Spain. She is our exotic and bold one. She is married to her high school sweetheart and they still live in Pine Bluff, Arkansas. She is elegant and beautiful. She and her husband regularly attend my annual *Go Deep Gathering*, which has meant the world to me. Her first grandbaby arrived this year and she is also smitten. She has become a great friend and I love her dearly.

I am number twelve of the YA YA's. I could not ask for a better group of lifetime friends. I wanted to talk about each one of them as they have all played a part in my life! I don't know of any friendships that have been together this long and still get together on a regular basis. They know the good, the bad, and the ugly, and we love each other very much! Great things come out of Pine Bluff, Arkansas.

So, this devotional is for them . . . and you, as this is my prayer:

*May the Lord make you hospitable like Debra, beautiful like Denise, smart like Sandy, disciplined like Cindy, give you a great memory like Jeanene, determined like Meredith, funny like Michelle, excellent like Carol, faithful like Jill, charming like Jeanne, sophisticated like Nancy and devoted like me.*

*May the Lord give you friendships that last a lifetime even when no words are spoken. May He envelop you with wisdom, knowledge and understanding enough to know that true happiness is in serving others and helping the least of these.*

*And most of all, may the Holy Spirit make Himself known to you so you hear the sound of His voice everyday so that you can go out and fulfill the destiny He has desired for you all along.*

*May we all be God's Dream Team together to reach a generation that mostly communicates by texts, only feels validated by the number of likes they have on social media, and has no idea that God is real and that He loves them more than words can say. May we somehow reach the lost and understand that everything we do should be driven by eternity so one day when we stand before our loving Father, He can say to us, "Well done my good and faithful servant, enter into my joy."*

*May the Lord richly bless you and give you wonderful lasting friendships.*

Liz Morris
Founder of *The Dallas Dream Team*

# Epilogue

*Come to me, all you who are weary and burdened,*
*and I will give you rest. Matthew 11:28*

Are you weary, burdened and feel like no one understands? We have all felt that way at one time or another. God knows what you are going through, and He is waiting with open arms for you to come to Him. Have you considered taking those burdens to Him? He tells us to come boldly to the throne of grace. Do not be afraid, you have a friend in Him, a friend who loves you. His love is unconditional. He loves you in spite of your faults, and He has your best interests in mind. Decide that you will not carry your burdens alone and trust Him. He loves you. He cannot and will not fail you.

Contributing Writer | Rosemary LeGrand

# NOTES

**Introduction | Liz Morris**

[1] *The Dallas Dream Team* awards financial grants to Christian 501c3 non-profits whose purpose is to serve people in need, proclaim the gospel and advance the Kingdom of God. We help these non-profits take an existing ministry program to a new level or help them launch a new initiative. We truly believe this allows the best impact of God's will to transform these lives. We are a group of ordinary women doing extraordinary things for the Kingdom of God. For more information, visit https://www.thedallasdreamteam.com.

**Attaining the Mind of Christ | Sheila Ninowski**

[2] Leaf, Dr. Caroline, *Who Switched Off My Brain, Controlling Toxic Thoughts and Emotions*, Nashville: Thomas Nelson Publishers, 2009.

**A Work in Progress | Carolyn Purdy**

[3] Lucado, Max, *Hermie the Caterpillar*, Nashville: Thomas Nelson Publishers, 2002.

Made in the USA
Columbia, SC
17 March 2021